D0527219

10

MINUTE GUIDE TO

HTML 4.0, THIRD EDITION

by Tim Evans

A Division of Macmillan Computer Publishing
201 West 103rd St., Indianapolis, Indiana 46290 USA

To C^2E, as always.

Copyright© 1998 by Que® Corporation.

Library of Congress Catalog No.: 97-69809

ISBN: 0-7897-1491-4

00 99 98   6 5 4 3 2 1

Interpretation of the printing code: The rightmost double-digit number is the year of the book's printing; the rightmost single-digit number, the number of the book's printing. For example, a printing code of 98-1 shows that the first printing of the book occurred in 1998.

Screen reproductions in this book were created using Collage Plus from Inner Media, Inc., Hollis, NH.

Composed in Stone Serif and Helvetica Light by Que Corporation.

CONTENTS

CREDITS

Senior Vice President of Publishing Richard K. Swadley

Publisher Jordan Gold

Manager of Publishing Operations Linda H. Buechler

General Manager Joe Muldoon

Director of Editorial Services Lisa Wilson

Director of Software and User Services Cheryl Willoughby

Managing Editor Patrick Kanouse

Indexing Manager Johnna L. VanHoose

Acquisitions Editor Jane Brownlow

Senior Product Director Lisa D. Wagner

Product Director Henly Wolin

Production Editor Julie A. McNamee

Product Marketing Manager Kourtnaye Sturgeon

Assistant Product Marketing Manager Gretchen Schlesinger

Technical Editors David Garratt, Stan Spink

Software Specialist David Garratt

Acquisitions Coordinator Tracy M. Williams

Software Relations Coordinator Susan D. Gallagher

Editorial Assistant Rhonda Tinch-Mize

Book Designers Ruth Harvey, Kim Scott

Cover Designer Sandra Schroeder

Production Team Juli Cook, Elizabeth Deeter, Sossity Smith, Becky Stutzman

Indexer Gregory Pearson

ABOUT THE AUTHORS

Tim Evans is the author of Que Publishing's *10 Minute Guide to Netscape for X Windows*, and Sams.net's *Building an Intranet*, as well as a UNIX system administration and network security consultant. Employed by Taratec Development Corporation, his full-time contract assignment for the past five years has been at the DuPont Company's Central Research and Development Department. He pioneered development of DuPont's own world-wide web, known as DuPont-Wide Web, widely used within the company for information sharing via its world-wide network. Besides this everyday assignment, he is responsible for Taratec's Internet services and is building a system-administration consultancy for the company. Previously, Tim worked for the U.S. Social Security Administration in various staff jobs for more than 20 years. In 1991, before the Internet got hot, he brought that government agency onto the Internet.

A native of Missouri, Tim has been a Carny, auto assembly line worker, janitor, bureaucrat, and bartender. His degrees in History show a Liberal Arts education can qualify you for almost any job, depending on what you do afterwards. Tim also is a produced playwright with an extensive background in community theatre, both on and off stage. His three produced stageplays were presented at a theatre on a street named "Broadway." He lives with his wife (and best friend) Carol in Delaware, just three hours from their vacation home in Chincoteague, VA. He can be reached via Internet e-mail at **tkevans@tkevans.com**.

ACKNOWLEDGEMENTS

Although this book is not in any way supported by the DuPont Company, Dr. David Pensak of the Company continues to inspire those who work for him to explore new computing technology. Without this encouragement and support when the World Wide Web was "new computing technology," this and the author's other books, would not have been possible. Thanks also to Jane Brownlow, Henly Wolin, and Julie McNamee of Que Publishing.

WE'D LIKE TO HEAR FROM YOU!

Que Corporation has a long-standing reputation for high-quality books and products. To ensure your continued satisfaction, we also understand the importance of customer service and support.

TECH SUPPORT

If you need assistance with the information in this book or with a CD/disk accompanying the book, please access Macmillan Computer Publishing's online Knowledge Base at **http://www. superlibrary.com/general/support**. If you do not find the answer to your questions on our Web site, you may contact Macmillan Technical Support by phone at **317/581-3833** or via e-mail at **support@mcp.com**.

Also be sure to visit Que's Web resource center for all the latest information, enhancements, errata, downloads, and more. It's located at **http://www.quecorp.com/**.

ORDERS, CATALOGS, AND CUSTOMER SERVICE

To order other Que or Macmillan Computer Publishing books, catalogs, or products, please contact our Customer Service Department at **800/428-5331** or fax us at **800/835-3202** (International Fax: 317/228-4400). Or visit our online bookstore at **http://www.mcp.com/**.

COMMENTS AND SUGGESTIONS

We want you to let us know what you like or dislike most about this book or other Que products. Your comments will help us to continue publishing the best books available on computer topics in today's market. Please contact

Henly Wolin
Product Director
Que Corporation
201 West 103rd Street, 4B
Indianapolis, Indiana 46290 USA
Fax: 317/581-4663 E-mail: ***hwolin@que.mcp.com***

Please be sure to include the book's title and author as well as your name and phone or fax number. We will carefully review your comments and share them with the author. Please note that due to the high volume of mail we receive, we may not be able to reply to every message.

Thank you for choosing Que!

INTRODUCTION

You've decided your organization needs to be on the World Wide Web, or your boss has made that decision, and given you the assignment of implementing it. Or you've decided it's time to join the legion of Internet users by creating a personal **home page** on the Web.

You've been accessing the Web for a while, and you probably have some ideas about how your company can make its products and services known on the Web, or how you can tell people about yourself with a home page. Now all you have to do is figure out how to put your ideas into HTML print, so to speak.

WHAT IS HTML?

The Hypertext Markup Language (HTML) is the language of the World Wide Web. HTML is part of the nuts and bolts of the Web. Every document on the Web is written in HTML, and all the document formatting, clickable hyperlinks, graphical images, jumping Java applets, multimedia documents, fill-in forms, and other Web hoo-haw you have seen are based on HTML.

Some people call HTML a programming language, but that's not correct. Rather, HTML is a simple, easy-to-learn **markup language**. Even novices can pick up the basics quickly. If you've learned to use your word processor, you've learned something more complex than HTML. All you need to do is get started.

WHAT IS THE 10 MINUTE GUIDE, AND WHY DO YOU NEED IT?

This book gives you that start. The *10 Minute Guide to HTML 4.0*, Third Edition uses a series of lessons that walk you through the basics of HTML, then moves on to more advanced features of the language. Each lesson is designed to take about 10 minutes, and each is limited to a particular feature, or several related features, of the HTML language. There are plenty of examples and screen shots to show you what things look like. By the time you finish the book, you'll be creating HTML documents rivaling any seen on the World Wide Web. You'll also be using HTML to provide unique and valuable services to your organization, or to tell the world about yourself. Who knows, this book might get you the promotion or personal recognition you've been waiting for.

Won't I Have to Learn Some Unfamiliar Computer System?

You can learn and use HTML on any computer system, including your desktop PC, using tools you're already familiar with. You're probably already using a Web browser like Netscape or Internet Explorer, and you'll learn in this book how to use it to preview and debug your HTML documents. We don't make any assumptions about the kind of computer system you're using in the book because HTML is completely system independent. Whether you're working on a Windows PC, a Macintosh, a high-performance UNIX workstation, or a multi-user VAX/VMS cluster, HTML is the same everywhere.

We do assume, though, that you have some basic computer skills, including the ability to use a word processor or basic text editor like the Windows Notepad, some basic understanding of directories and file names on your computer system, and some experience with a Web browser like Netscape or Internet Explorer. Some HTML features require a bit of programming experience of some kind, although the basics of the scripting languages—JavaScript and VBScript—are quite easy to pick up.

HTML Standards

The HTML 4.0 draft standards were issued in mid-1997—one year after the HTML 3.2 standards—and may have become final by the time you read this. Prior to HTML 4.0, development of the language ran at a breakneck pace, fueled by fierce competition between Microsoft and Netscape. Each company added new features to its Web browsers and then extended HTML to support them. As a result, there was a divergence in HTML that created headaches for HTML authors.

HTML 4.0 brings some measure of respite in this area, with most of both companies' added features brought into the standard. Both Netscape and Microsoft promptly endorsed the new draft standard, promising to bring their Web browsers into compliance.

The future of HTML is not, however, as rosy as you might think. Microsoft and Netscape remain locked in a battle for the hearts, minds, and Web browsers of millions of you. Even with the endorsement of HTML 4.0 by both companies, you can still expect new developments in HTML. Furthermore, in some respects, the new standard merely institutionalizes differences in HTML features between the two major camps. You'll still need to be aware of these differences. This *10 Minute Guide* will highlight those differences.

Still HTML 4.0 is a great improvement over the earlier situation, and it makes learning HTML easier.

Special Icons

In addition to the explanatory text and many sets of cookbook-style steps in this book, you will find icons that highlight special kinds of information.

Plain English sidebars appear whenever a new term is defined. If you aren't familiar with terms and concepts, watch for these flagged paragraphs.

Panic Button sidebars alert you to common mistakes and tell you how to avoid them. These paragraphs also explain how to undo certain features, and highlight remaining differences in HTML.

> **TIP**   Timesaver Tip sidebars explain shortcuts (for example, key combinations) for performing certain tasks.

CONVENTIONS USED IN THE BOOK

The creation and editing of HTML documents can be done using any of a wide variety of editing tools. As a result, this book doesn't use the "press-this-key" or "type-in-this-command" format common in the *10 Minute Guide* series. Rather, you'll find many excerpts from HTML documents that illustrate points being made. These fragments look like this:

<HTML><HEAD><TITLE>Title of Document</TITLE>
</HEAD><BODY>Some Text and HTML Markup Code
</BODY></HTML>

If you're working along with the examples, you may want to enter the HTML fragments into your own HTML documents as you work through the lessons.

Some easy-to-identify elements throughout the book:

What you type/ HTML fragments	HTML examples and excerpts you can type appear in **bold** type.
New/Important terms	Terms you should pay special attention to also appear in **bold** type.

THE SCREEN SHOTS IN THIS BOOK

A wide variety of Web browsers were used for the screen shots in this book. While many are shots of the latest available releases of Netscape Navigator and Microsoft Internet Explorer, others are of older browsers on various computer systems. This is done on purpose since the book is about HTML, not about Web browsers. This variety of screen shots underscores the fact that HTML works pretty much the same in all Web browsers. Of course, where new or unique HTML features are described, screen shots showing the appropriate browsers are provided.

OVERVIEW OF HTML

In this lesson, you learn what you can and can't do with HTML.

ADVANTAGES OF HTML

The Hypertext Markup Language is the language of the World Wide Web. Every time you access a Web document, you're accessing a document someone wrote in HTML. All the document formatting you see in Web documents is done with HTML, and the hyperlinks you follow so easily by clicking with your mouse are set up using HTML, too. Those colorful animated images you see on the Web, those flashy forms you've filled in, and those jumping Java applets are also products of the HTML language you'll learn in this book. HTML is easy to learn, and by the time you've finished the lessons in this book, you'll be creating professional-quality HTML documents.

Here's a short list of the major features of HTML:

- **Document formatting** using various typeface styles, a range of headlines, and a new feature called Frames.

- The capability to include **hyperlinks** that point to other Web documents, multimedia files, or services on computer systems all over the Internet.

- A wide range of **list layout** capabilities.

- The capability to create **tables** and **preformatted text**.

- The capability to **embed graphical images** right in an HTML document, which can be hyperlinked to other documents.

- **Clickable image maps** with hot spots to take you various places depending on where in the image you've clicked.

- Inclusion of **interactive features** such as fill-in forms and programs that involve the user.

- **Active Web pages**, which feature downloadable application programs that run on your own computer.

You've probably seen all these features and more on the Web. In this book, you'll learn how to create your own HTML documents, which include these same features. Whether you're learning because your company or organization wants to go on the Web or just because you're curious, we'll cover the basics of this language.

LIMITATIONS OF HTML

Before we go into the nuts and bolts of HTML, however, you need to know some fundamental limitations of the language, not to discourage you from learning and using it, but to give you an overall perspective on what you can expect.

NOT A TYPESETTING LANGUAGE

Most of the changes in HTML, including those in HTML 4.0, have been directed at giving Web page designers more control over the appearance of HTML pages. Accordingly, improvements have given you enhanced ability to control line spacing and justification, typeface size and fonts, HTML tables, graphical image placement, and the flow of text around images. Nevertheless, HTML is still not a full-blown typesetting language; it can't deal with complex mathematical expressions or scientific notation, for example.

As a result, what your HTML documents look like when people view them still isn't subject to your total control, as it would be in printed documents. And you can lead a user to a graphical image, but he won't necessarily look at it; many users who use slow links to the Internet disable image display to speed up downloads.

PHYSICAL DIFFERENCES IN HARDWARE

Hardware differences are the most important limitation affecting HTML. Your PC may have a nice, color monitor with a 14-inch screen, but the engineers in your company probably have higher resolution, 24-inch screens on high-end Sun workstations for their CAD design, your graphic designers may have high-end PowerMacs, and the folks in the back office use PCs with monochrome screens, or even dumb terminals, to do word processing or data entry. Every one of these pieces of hardware has different capabilities, yet each one is potentially capable of accessing the World Wide Web and looking at your documents written in HTML.

Dumb Terminals   Minimal-capability computer terminal screens with keyboards. They often don't display color or any kind of graphics—just letters and other characters.

You don't expect monochrome displays to deal with color, you can't expect low-resolution displays to render graphical images well, and those dumb terminals can't do anything but display plain text in just one boring, fixed font. Color and type fonts differ as well. These physical differences mean your HTML documents get rendered differently from PC to workstation to terminal.

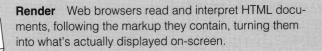

Render   Web browsers read and interpret HTML documents, following the markup they contain, turning them into what's actually displayed on-screen.

CHOOSING PERSONAL PREFERENCES

If you've "played on the Web" very much, you've probably noticed your Web browser has some **user-settable features**. You can, for instance, select from a range of font styles and sizes available on your system, based purely on your personal preferences. Also, you can set your browser to delay the loading and display of images in an HTML document. If you do, the HTML author's images are replaced by generic placeholders that can be clicked to reveal the original image. This feature is designed to minimize the time it takes to load and render a document and is of most benefit to users whose network connections are over slow, dial-up links. (See Lesson 11, "Adding Images to Your Document," for more on this problem.) Finally, when you resize your Web browser display, the documents you view take the new size of the display. In some cases, resizing the window will cause the document's text to be reformatted to fit the new window size, with different line breaks.

Taken together, user preferences can radically alter the on-screen appearance of your Web pages. For instance, you can use different fonts and reformat paragraph layout.

VIEWING HTML DOCUMENTS IN DIFFERENT BROWSERS

Viewing your HTML documents in different Web browsers can give you a better feel for the differences.

New changes in the HTML language and the way browsers interpret it have removed many early limitations, but, as you can see, some remain. Do these limitations mean you shouldn't bother to learn HTML? Before you answer that question, remember all the Web surfing you've done and how impressed you've been with what you've seen. The HTML language, despite its remaining limitations (a list that is continually shrinking), is highly capable and you'll agree its capabilities outweigh its limitations. This book shows you how to get the most out of HTML.

One way of working with these limitations is to think of your documents not in terms of physical things, like where the lines break or specific font styles, but rather in a larger, more general sense. It's also important to remember it's the **content** of your documents that gives them value, and not necessarily the **presentation**, important though the latter may be.

We've introduced the Hypertext Markup Language in this lesson. Even with the limitations we've mentioned, you can achieve impressive things with HTML. Before we get into HTML specifics, the next couple of lessons introduce World Wide Web server and browser software, respectively, in the context of HTML.

UNDERSTANDING WEB SERVERS

In this lesson, you learn about World Wide Web server software packages.

WHY IS A SERVER IMPORTANT?

A World Wide Web server delivers your HTML documents to the people who want to look at them. Without servers, there would be no Web and no need for HTML.

Even if you've decided to hire a professional Web service provider to run a Web server on your behalf, you need to know some server basics in order to understand what you're doing when you write HTML documents.

THE HTTP NETWORK PROTOCOL

The World Wide Web operates on computer networks which run the **Internet Protocols** (also called **TCP/IP—Transmission Control Protocol/Internet Protocols**).

> **Internet Protocol** Mathematical equations are a good analogy. Equations are made up of combinations of symbols from a universally agreed-to set of symbols. New symbols are not allowed and the rules for using them are very specific. Network protocols work in exactly this way. Like trained mathematicians, computer programmers use a specific, agreed-to vocabulary of symbols to insure precise and understandable communications.

Web **browsers**, like Internet Explorer or Netscape, communicate over a network (including the Internet) with Web **servers**, using

the **http (HyperText Transfer Protocol)**, as illustrated in
Figure 2.1. Browsers send network requests to servers, asking that:

- Specific documents or services be provided by the server.
  The server returns the document or service if it's available, also using the http protocol, and the browser receives and understands it.

- Web servers run programs based on information you enter in fill-in forms, such as placing orders, accessing database applications, or sending electronic mail. Your
  browser receives and interprets the results of the
  program's run.

- Web servers allow you to download software, such as
  updated Web browsers, to your computer.

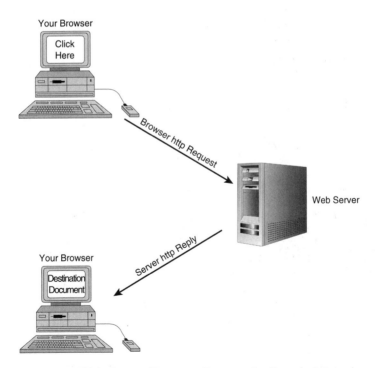

FIGURE 2.1 Web Server/Browser Communication via http.

The **Hypertext Markup Language**, which you're learning in this book, is one part of the precise set of symbols that make up the http protocol.

HTTP AND OTHER INTERNET PROTOCOLS

There are many network protocols spoken on the Internet, each one for a specific and limited purpose, such as electronic mail or file transfers. You may also have heard of other services like *Gopher*, *Telnet*, and *WAIS*. Each of these protocols works well for its own purpose, and you can use programs on your computer which communicate by using them to locate and retrieve information on the Net.

Each one of these programs, however, works differently and has a different user interface, leading to a good deal of confusion on the part of new Internet users. Assuming you can find the data you want, which program do you use to access it? And where did you put the obscure set of instructions for this particular program?

The http protocol was designed to incorporate many network protocols into a single, multi-purpose protocol. What's important to the World Wide Web user is Web browsers speak the http protocol: The user can access a wide variety of network services just by pointing and clicking. Using http, the Web browser takes care of locating, retrieving, and, most importantly, interpreting the data.

What's specifically important to you, the HTML author, is your HTML documents contain various kinds of **markup**, including pointers to the Web and other Internet services. Your **hyperlinks** tell the user's Web browser how to access and retrieve the data you've made available. As you'll learn in the upcoming lessons, the HTML language is made up of a specific set of rules and symbols that are part of http.

Markup HTML documents contain special markup symbols for document formatting, links, and other things you'll learn in the following lessons.

Hyperlinks The highlighted words and phrases found in World Wide Web documents you can click to jump to another document or Internet service.

WORLD WIDE WEB SERVER SOFTWARE

World Wide Web server software is available for a variety of computer systems, in both no-cost and commercial packages. A few are mentioned in the following sections.

UNIX SOFTWARE

The http protocol and the Web servers and clients which use it were initially developed in Switzerland at CERN, the European Particle Physics Lab, though "**httpd**" development has moved elsewhere. "**Http**" becomes "**httpd**" in this context; UNIX server programs are frequently referred to as "**daemons**," hence, the "d" in httpd reflects the daemon, or server software.

Two no-cost **httpd** servers dominate the UNIX Web server market, with a number of commercial packages also available. The most widely used free UNIX httpd server is called **Apache** (**http://www.apache.org/**). Apache is based on the now-defunct **NCSA** (National Center for Supercomputing Applications) server. Though still widely used, the NCSA server is no longer being developed or maintained. Most recent UNIX releases, including Sun's Solaris 2.6, IBM's AIX 4.x, and others, bundle

Web server software at no extra cost. Netscape Communications Corporation, makers of the Netscape Navigator Web browser, is a major marketer of commercial httpd servers for UNIX systems

If you are concerned about the security of your network and have installed a network **firewall**, you'll want to use the Apache or Netscape servers (or even the original CERN server, now maintained by the World Wide Web Consortium, W[3]). These packages have a **proxy** mode which allows you to set things up so your network remains protected by your firewall, but your users can still access the Web through the proxy server.

Firewall   A network firewall isolates your network from the outside world for security reasons, permitting only approved network traffic to pass between your network and the outside. While the primary purpose of a firewall is to protect your own network, it may also be used to limit your access to the outside world and other networks in your company.

Proxy   When your network is protected by a firewall, it's often necessary for a proxy httpd server to retrieve Web pages for you from the outside world and relay them through the firewall to your computer. Web browsers must be told to use the proxy server, usually in the browser's *Preferences* or *Options* dialog box.

WEB SERVER SOFTWARE FOR PCS

You don't need a UNIX computer system to set up and run a World Wide Web server. Modern PCs will also do, but it's important to distinguish between *general* and *personal* Web servers. The latter is a Web server you'd run on your own PC—the one in Windows 98, for example—for just your own Web pages. Personal

Web servers should be thought of as just that, and not used for your company's (or even your Department's) main Web server.

> **Network Connections Limits** Windows NT 4.0 Workstation includes a Web server package, *Peer Web Services*, but Windows NT Workstation has a hard-coded limit of 10 simultaneous network connections. This is actually a *licensing* limit that applies to even the fastest, most powerful PC, and it's built into Windows NT. Since this limit applies across the board to all network connections, you'll find Windows NT Workstation a bad choice for anything other than a personal Web server. It seems reasonable to expect the built-in Windows 98 *Personal Web Server* to have similar limitations. If you need to run a general Web server on NT, you'll need to spring for the *Server* version of NT.

Http server software is available for IBM-compatible PCs running Microsoft Windows and OS/2 and for Macintosh computers. In the former category, software based on the NCSA httpd server is available for Windows PCs in a shareware version. A very large number of free and commercial packages are available for Windows NT, including **Internet Information Server,** (IIS). The Apache server for Windows NT was in alpha test at the time this book was being written, and may be available in a usable version by the time you read this. IBM's **Internet Connection Server** (commercial) is available for PCs running OS/2. For the Macintosh, the commercial package of choice is **MACHTTPD**, while freeware packages include **httpd4Mac** and **EasyServe**.

You'll want to be careful in selecting a PC on which to run an http server. Older operating systems, such as Windows 3.1 or MacOS releases prior to release 7, do a less-than-outstanding job of **multi-tasking** (essential for Web servers, which must be able to respond to many http requests in a short time). If you choose a PC or Mac for a server platform, you'll probably want to dedicate a high-end machine to this task and make sure its operating system is up to date, rather than trying to run a server on somebody's desktop PC while it's in everyday office use. For IBM-compatible PCs, you'll probably want to run Windows NT, which does true, pre-emptive multi-tasking; Windows NT 4.0 Server includes Microsoft's IIS Web server software at no extra charge. As noted above, Windows 98 may not be a good choice except for personal Web servers.

A good alternative to Windows httpd servers for IBM-compatible PCs is not to run Windows at all. Rather, try a PC version of UNIX, such as Solaris, BSDI, Esix, SCO UNIX, or even—if you're up to it—one of the freeware UNIX lookalikes, Linux or FreeBSD. All these systems either include bundled Web server software or can be used to build and run the Apache server package. Since UNIX is a true multi-tasking operating system, potential problems in running and managing a Web server are avoided. PCs that are, by today's standards, low-end (such as an early Pentium, or even a 486) can comfortably run a Web server under UNIX, and are not subject to connection limits. On a Mac, you can get around the same problems with Apple's MacOS Version 8—a UNIX derivitive—or with the still-developing port of Linux to the PowerMac architecture.

COMMERCIAL WEB SERVER SOFTWARE

As you might guess, demand for httpd server software is high, and a number of companies sell commercial Web server software, most prominently the Netscape servers for UNIX and NT systems, O'Reilly and Associates' **WebSite** server for Windows NT, and the **MACHTTPD** server from StarNine. There's an always up-to-date Web server comparison chart on the Web at **http://www. webcompare.com/**.

These commercially developed server software packages have features above and beyond the free server software we've described. These features include:

- **Encryption** of sensitive information (such as credit card numbers and other personal or business information).

- **Authentication** of users accessing the server to ensure confidentiality.

- Enhanced **tracking** of who accesses the server.

- Tracking of **data retrievals**, so software and other data can actually be sold interactively over the Net.

Need Some Support?   Of course, you should also be able to expect commercial-grade support from Web server software vendors. This is a potentially critical matter, especially if you don't have in-house expertise in managing the software. "Free" software packages are invariably not free when you have to provide your own support.

In this lesson, you've learned some essential information about World Wide Web server software. We've discussed the http network protocol and its inclusion of other Internet protocols, which allow Web browser software to easily and quickly locate and retrieve many kinds of data. Finally, we've discussed several Web httpd server software packages. In the next lesson, we'll learn about World Wide Web browser software.

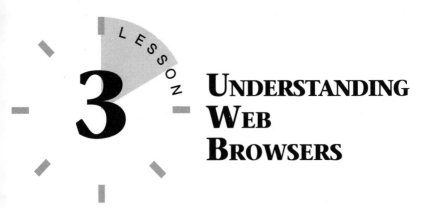

UNDERSTANDING WEB BROWSERS

In this lesson, you learn about the various World Wide Web browser software packages and how they deal with HTML documents.

WHY DO I NEED A BROWSER?

The short answer to this question is that you need a browser to "get on the Web." That is, to get to the vast amount of information on the World Wide Web, you need a computer program, usually called a Web browser.

Because you're probably already accessing the Web, this is old news. You're reading this book because you want to learn the HTML language, which is at the heart of the Web. Look at what happens when you click a hyperlink:

1. Your browser has read a document written in the HTML language and displayed it for you, rendering (interpreting) all the markup codes in it.

2. When you click the hyperlink, your browser uses the HTTP protocol to send a network request to a Web server for the document or service specified by the HTML hyperlink.

3. The Web server responds to the requests, also using the HTTP protocol, with the document or other data you requested.

4. Your browser software then reads and interprets that information, often written in HTML, and presents it to you in its version of the correct format.

As you can see from this list and Figure 3.1, what goes on when you click a hyperlink is a pretty significant series of events, involving not only your Web browser software, but also a Web server somewhere, and the transactions involved rely heavily on the HTML language.

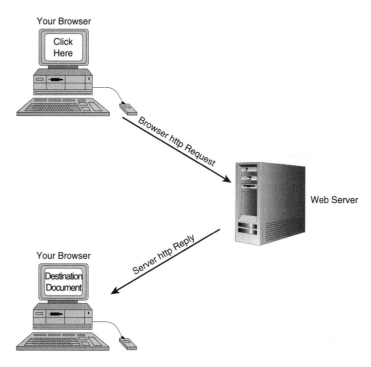

FIGURE 3.1   Web browser/server communication.

SURVEY OF WEB BROWSER SOFTWARE

You can choose from many Web browser software packages. All have in common their use of HTML and the HTTP protocol. Also, the transactions they conduct follow much the same lines as those listed in the previous section. As Web browsers have developed over the past several years, more and more new features were added. To support these new features, HTML has grown and changed, accelerated by competition between Microsoft and Netscape. The HTML 4.0 standard is the current state of the language, but you can expect more changes.

Although the primary subject of this book is HTML, not browsers, let's take a quick look at some of the most widely used browsers.

NETSCAPE NAVIGATOR

Netscape Navigator is a commercial Web browser from Netscape Communications Corporation. It remains the most widely used Web browser. Netscape runs on UNIX systems, PCs, and Macs. Netscape has pioneered some important browser improvements, especially in the area of optimizing performance over dial-up telephone (modem) links, and has also done much work in extending HTML standards.

In addition, Netscape has commercial Web server software available, which has significant improvements and new features, especially in the area of secure/confidential Web transactions.

You can obtain evaluation copies of Netscape at no cost on the Web at **http://home.netscape.com**. If you're in an educational or nonprofit institution or just want to use Netscape for personal purposes, Netscape is free, but others must pay for the package beyond an initial evaluation period. Licensed users of Netscape are allowed to make a copy of the package for home use. Figure 3.2 shows a Web page displayed with Netscape version 3. Netscape Communicator, an integrated package of Internet/Web applications including Netscape Navigator version 4, is the current release.

Version differences   You may want to compare Figure 3.2 with Figure 1.1 in Lesson 1, so you can see the differences between Netscape versions 3 and 4. As noted earlier, this book uses a variety of Web browsers to illustrate HTML.

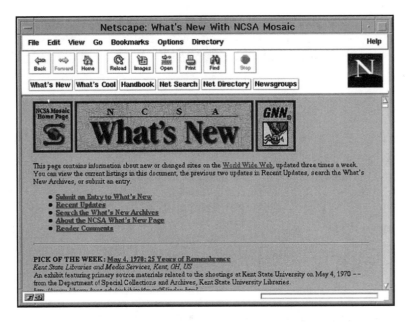

FIGURE 3.2   Netscape Navigator version 3.

MICROSOFT INTERNET EXPLORER

Bill Gates has brought all his considerable resources into the Web browser fray with Internet Explorer, including many new features. **MSIE** has seriously eroded Netscape's market lead. Version 4 was released in the Fall of 1997. The new version is tightly integrated into the Windows desktop. Internet Explorer also runs on Macintosh PCs (though the release level tends to lag). In addition, Microsoft has been promising a UNIX version of IE for more than a year, with the latest target date being the first quarter of 1998. Figure 3.3 shows Internet Explorer version 4. You can download Internet Explorer free at **http://www.microsoft.com/ie/**.

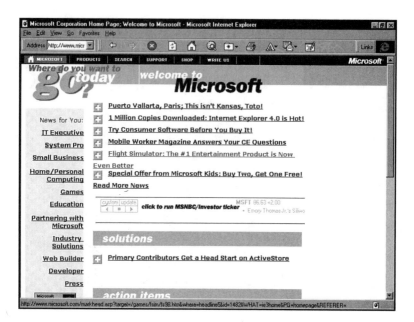

FIGURE 3.3   Microsoft Internet Explorer.

Mosaic   Internet Explorer is based on the first graphical Web browser, **NCSA Mosaic**. Mosaic was developed at the National Center for Supercomputing Applications at the University of Illinois, primarily by Mark Andreesen, co-founder of Netscape Communications Corporation. Although it wasn't the first Web browser, it was the first browser with the **point-and-click graphical user interface**. Mosaic is no longer supported by NCSA, although some commercially enhanced versions remain in use.

OTHER BROWSERS

Despite, or perhaps because of, the near-total domination of the Web browser market by Netscape and Microsoft, literally dozens of other Web browsers are available. Many are free or shareware, although most are commercial packages. The basic free NCSA

Mosaic browser remains available; several vendors have licensed it for commercial enhancement and resale through Spyglass, Inc. The major online services (CompuServe, America Online, and so on) all have browsers for their customers, although the list of other available packages is too long to include here.

Windows 98   Microsoft's next release of Windows, Windows 98 (also known as Memphis) went into beta test in the summer of 1997. This will be a fundamental change in Windows, because the Microsoft **Active Desktop** graphical interface becomes the main interface to both the local Windows system and the Internet. In other words, you'll use the IE browser/Active Desktop as the single interface to both the Internet and all your local programs files. Windows 98 will also include a Personal Web Server, which will enable you to publish Web pages right on your PC.

You'll find a terrific Web browser comparison chart on the Web at *Browser Blvd*, **http://browserwatch.internet.com/browsers.html**. This chart includes feature listings, operating systems supported, and the like, and also contains links to browser vendor Web sites, many of which enable demo copies of their software to be downloaded.

Considering Servers   If you're setting up a Web server for your company's customers, you might want to license Spyglass Enhanced Mosaic, Netscape, or Internet Explorer for redistribution and simply hand out copies to your customers, preconfigured to access your Web server at startup.

TIP

As a student of HTML, you might be particularly interested in the **Amaya** browser, being developed by the World Wide Web Consortium, or W³C. The whole purpose of **Amaya** is to provide a test bed for HTML standards development. Figure 3.4 shows the Amaya Web browser.

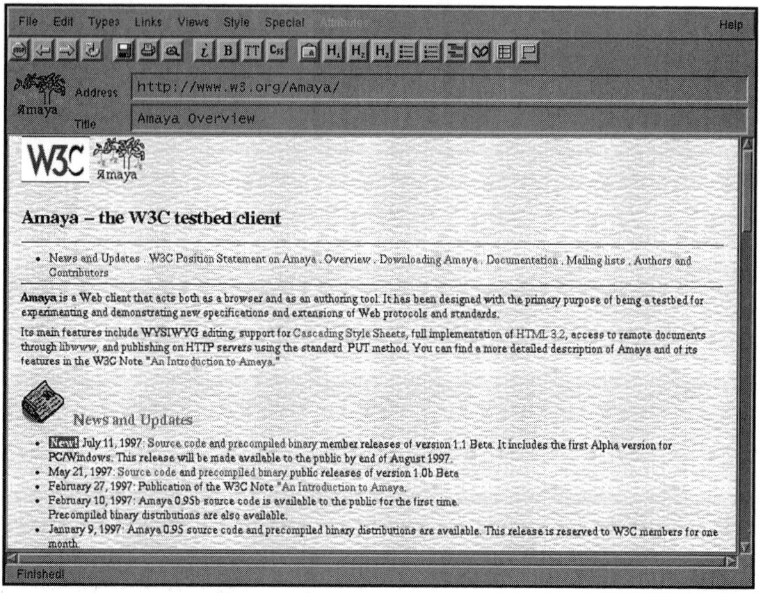

FIGURE 3.4   Amaya browser.

> **W³C**   This is an industry consortium that develops common standards for the evolution of the Web by producing specifications and reference software. The HTML 4.0 standard was developed by W³C.

NONGRAPHICAL WEB BROWSERS

Most of us are lucky enough to have computers that support graphical Web browsers, but some people live in a character-based terminal world. Users of older PCs may not have Windows, and many organizations support users with dumb terminals that have little or no graphical features. These users, of course, can't run the graphical Web browser software we've described so far.

Dumb terminals   These are minimal-capability computer screens with keyboards. They don't display color, or any kind of graphics—just letters and other characters.

Fortunately, for these folks, nongraphical browsers, also called plain-text browsers, are available. They don't have all the bells and whistles that Internet Explorer or Netscape have, but they get the job done.

Most widely used is the **Lynx** package, freeware originally from the University of Kansas. It is available for UNIX systems, VAX/ VMS systems, and PCs (including Macs, Amigas and even Ataris). Lynx can be downloaded from its main page, **http:// www.crl.com/~subir/lynx/**. Figure 3.5 shows the Lynx browser running on a UNIX system.

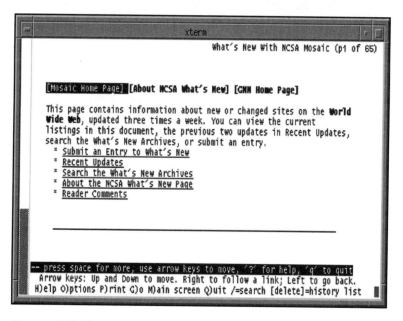

FIGURE 3.5   Lynx nongraphical browser.

WEB HELPER APPLICATIONS

Before we close this lesson, you need to learn about **Helper ap-plications**. The Web browsers we've mentioned are pretty con-sistent in the types of data they can interpret correctly. This includes, as you'll learn in upcoming lessons, certain types of graphical images, HTML documents, plain text files, and common Internet protocols. There's a whole range of types of data, how-ever, that Web browsers don't handle by themselves.

Fortunately, the designers of the first Web browsers—the folks at CERN and those at NCSA—came up with a way for other kinds of data to be handled by Web browsers. Web browsers can be set up so that, when they encounter a kind of data they can't handle by themselves, they'll hand it off to an external, **Helper** application.

Helper Applications   These are applications that take the data Web browsers can't interpret and deal with it, displaying unsupported images or playing sound or video files.

For example, you'll learn in Lesson 13, "Helper Applications and Plug-Ins for Multimedia," that you can include hyperlinks in your HTML documents pointing to sound, video, and many other kinds of datafiles. This mechanism is so flexible that you can set up your Web server with, say, Excel spreadsheet datafiles or WordPerfect documents and configure your Web browser so that it automatically fires up Excel or WordPerfect when you click a hyperlink pointing to one of those files. Think of the possibilities of this, even if your Web is limited to your own company network.

PLUG-INS

Netscape extended and expanded the Helper applications concept with its **plug-in** feature; other recent browsers have adopted the concept as well. Although traditional Web browser Helper applications usually open a new window to display a movie, for example, plug-ins enable the movie to be played right within the Netscape window.

Netscape Communications Corporation made public the software specifications for creating plug-ins, and many other software vendors are creating software packages that work as Netscape plug-ins. This is a fast-moving area, so you'll want to check the latest plug-in news on the Web. Using Netscape, just pull down the **Help** menu and select **About Plug-ins**, or go directly to the plug-ins page at **http://home.netscape.com/comprod/ products/version_2.0/plugins/**. As noted, Internet Explorer supports Netscape-style plug-ins.

JAVA APPLETS AND ACTIVEX CONTROLS

More recent than Helper Applications and Plug-ins, Java applets and ActiveX controls are small computer programs that download when they are accessed by using a Web browser and run on your own computer. You'll learn more about Java and ActiveX in Lesson 17, "Active Web Pages with Java and ActiveX."

This lesson explained the basics of the way Web browsers work to read documents written in HTML and retrieve and interpret data from Web servers using the HTTP protocol. We surveyed the available Web browser software and discussed browser Helper applications, Netscape plug-ins, and applets for dealing with data your browser can't handle. In the next lesson, we'll get down to the business of HTML.

4 CREATING A SIMPLE HTML DOCUMENT

LESSON

In this lesson, you create your first HTML document. Also, you learn that you can use familiar tools already on your computer system to create and edit HTML documents.

WHAT TOOLS DO YOU NEED?

HTML documents are **plain text** (**ASCII**) with special markup codes embedded right in the text. This means HTML files contain nothing but plain letters, numbers, punctuation marks, and other printable characters—including HTML markup codes. They can be read or printed directly by your computer's operating system commands.

Although some specialized tools for creating and editing HTML documents are available (we'll look at them in Lesson 21, "HTML Editors"), you can begin creating HTML immediately with tools you already have on hand. These include the following:

- Your computer's built-in text editors, such as the Microsoft Windows *Notepad*, Windows 95 *WordPad*, DOS *edit* or *edlin*, Windows *Write*, Macintosh *TeachText/ SimpleText*, UNIX *vi* or *emacs*, or VAX/VMS *edt*.

- Your favorite word processor, such as Microsoft Word, WordPerfect, or any other package you use, used in plain text or ASCII mode.

In fact, you can use whatever tool with which you're comfortable for creating documents, making the HTML learning process much less of a chore. You can focus on learning and creating HTML, without having to learn a special tool at the same time.

Select whatever editor you're going to use to create your HTML document. The examples in this book show the Windows Notepad, Windows 95 WordPad, and the UNIX vi editors, but you can use any text editor that can create and edit plain ASCII text files. If you're using a regular word processor, such as Microsoft Word, WordPerfect, or Write, be sure to use the **Save As** feature to save the documents in plain ASCII text.

Direct Editing   Recent releases of the major word processors, including both Microsoft Word and Corel WordPerfect, enable you to create and edit HTML documents directly. For the time being, we'll ignore these capabilities, but you will learn about them in Lesson 21.

TIP   **Use the Extension**   Although it's not required, it's a good idea to use the .html (or .htm on older PC operating systems, such as DOS or Windows 3.x) file name extension when saving HTML documents. Later, you'll be able to tell the kind of documents they are.

You may want to bring up an empty document in your chosen editor and follow along with this lesson.

WHAT DOES HTML LOOK LIKE?

The factor that distinguishes an HTML file from any other plain-text file is the presence of simple *markup codes*, called HTML **tags**. These codes are typed right into a document; they control the formatting and layout of your finished document, specify hyperlinks to other documents, and other things we'll cover. Web browsers read HTML markup and **render** the HTML document on-screen.

HTML markup codes are surrounded by special markers to set them off from the substantive text of the document. You just type them right in, using HTML's two key symbols to signal markup instructions. These symbols are the **angle brackets**, < and >. (Type these characters on most computer keyboards by using Shift+, (comma) and Shift+. (period).)

An important thing to note about HTML markup codes is they are *not case-sensitive*. <body> is the same as <bODy> or <boDy> or <BodY>. Many HTML authors use uppercase consistently for HTML markup codes because it makes the markup stand out visually from the actual text of the HTML document, easing the chore of proofreading.

WHAT HTML TAGS ARE REQUIRED IN DOCUMENTS?

Let's start by noting basic HTML tags that must appear in all HTML documents. These include the following:

- A declaration of the fact that your document is an HTML document

- A title

- Some tags that divide your document into logical parts

Logical Parts?   Different Web browsers render your HTML documents in different ways—color, type fonts, size, and so on—requiring you to think of your documents as logical entities, not physical ones, bearing in mind that the physical look may vary from one viewer to another and from one computer to another. The basic HTML markup tags you'll learn in this lesson divide individual documents into logical parts, or sections.

THE <HTML> TAG

Every HTML document must begin and end with the **<HTML>** tag, declaring the document an HTML document. No matter what else your HTML document contains, it must contain these tags. The HTML markup tag pair looks like this:

<HTML>

My First HTML Document

</HTML>

Always wrap your HTML documents with the beginning and ending **<HTML>** tags.

> **TIP**
>
> **Forward Slash**   Many HTML tags come in pairs, and the closing pair always requires the forward slash, corresponding with the opening tag, as shown in the example.

THE **<HEAD>** AND **<BODY>** TAGS

All HTML documents are divided into two parts—the **head** and **body**. Web browsers distinguish between them to interpret your documents properly. Generally speaking, the head part of an HTML document includes general information *about* the document, and the body is its actual content. For now, we're focusing on the body of your documents; you'll learn about the meta-information that may go into the head section in Lesson 23, "Other Aspects of HTML 4.0."

Let's extend the above example to include <HEAD> tags.

<HTML><HEAD>

...the matter making up the head section

</HEAD>

My First HTML Document</HTML>

As you can see from the addition of the pair of <HEAD> tags here (including the forward slash on the closing tag), HTML tags can appear on the same line with other tags.

Next, we'll add the <BODY> tags to complete the logical division of your document; all HTML documents must have both a <HEAD> and a <BODY> section:

<HTML><HEAD>

...the matter making up the head section

</HEAD><BODY>

My First HTML Document

</BODY></HTML>

The following summarizes what you've learned so far:

- Your document begins and ends with <HTML> start and stop tags.

- Your document is divided into two sections, marked off with the <HEAD> and <BODY> tags, which are nested inside the overall pair of <HTML> tags.

- Each of these tags comes in pairs: <HTML> and </HTML>; <HEAD> and </HEAD>; and <BODY> and </BODY>.

The <TITLE> Tag

<TITLE> is the last required HTML tag. As you've noticed while using the Web, your Web browser usually displays a title for each document it encounters, most often in the top border of your browser window. The title displayed is taken from the content of the <TITLE> tag in the HTML document.

> **No Title** While you've learned the <TITLE> tag is mandatory in HTML documents, you will no doubt find Web pages on the Internet that don't have them. This shows that Web browsers are usually quite permissive when they encounter mistakes or missing HTML tags. Nonetheless, your HTML documents should always have a <TITLE> tag.

Always appearing *within the <HEAD> section* of your HTML document, <TITLE> also comes in pairs, surrounding the text you've entered as the title of your document. Let's make one last change to our example document to add these tags:

<HTML><HEAD><TITLE>The Title of the Document</TITLE>

</HEAD><BODY>

My First HTML Document

</BODY></HTML>

Our HTML document is now complete, containing all the tags an HTML document must have. In fact, the document is a legal HTML document, and you can view it in your Web browser.

Pretty basic document, isn't it? Well, yes, it is, but you've just completed your first HTML document.

If you've been working along in your own editor, now's the time to save your document, just as you'd save any other document. The required HTML markup tags make your document an HTML document. If you're using a regular word processor, don't forget to save it in plain text. Use **First.htm** for a file name. Using a Web browser, you can now take a look at the document.

DISPLAYING AND PREVIEWING YOUR HTML DOCUMENT

You know you can use your Web browser to view documents from Web servers across the Internet, but you may not realize you can use the same browser to view documents on your own computer system. This is a critical part of your work in creating HTML documents because it enables you to preview, and debug, your documents before letting anyone else see them.

To view a local HTML document with Internet Explorer version 4:

1. Pull down the **File** menu and select **Open.**

2. You see a dialog box. Click **Browse** and locate your file, *First.htm*, then select it.

Your Web browser brings up your HTML document. Figure 4.1 illustrates the process of opening a local document for preview in IE 4.0.

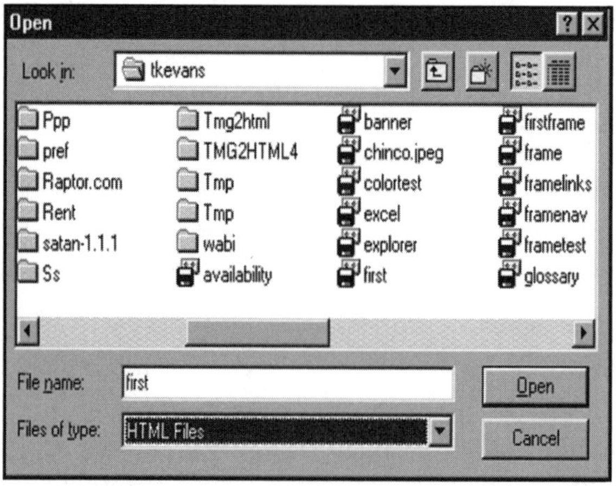

FIGURE 4.1   Loading the local document for preview in Internet Explorer 4.0.

> **Same Feature, Different Place**   These instructions apply to Internet Explorer; all other browsers have the capability to preview files on your computer, but it may be in a different place or use slightly different wording. Netscape version 4 uses **Open Page**, for example. Earlier browsers have an explicit **Open File** item on the File menu. See your browser's documentation or help files.

If you've typed in the HTML document you've been working on in this lesson, the display in your Web browser should be much like Figure 4.2. Of course, this document is pretty plain. You see the title of the document displayed in the Title bar, and the one line of text you've entered.

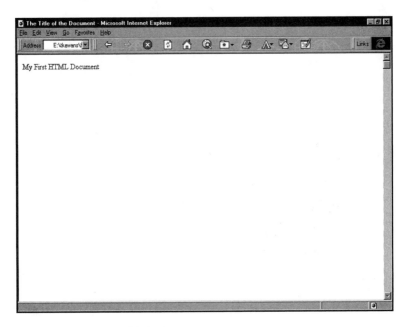

FIGURE 4.2   First HTML document.

HTML documents are plain-text documents with markup tags. They can be created with just about any editing tool you may have, including text editors or your favorite word processor. HTML documents must have the four tags we've discussed in this lesson. Each tag must be paired with its closing tag.

In the next lesson, we'll extend what you've learned about basic HTML markup by learning about typeface styles and paragraphing.

5 INTRODUCTION TO HTML STYLE SHEETS

In this lesson, you'll learn about style sheets, probably the most important aspect of HTML 4.0, and how using them helps in the creation of your HTML documents.

MOST IMPORTANT ASPECT OF HTML 4.0

Although the uneasy peace in HTML 4.0 over the issue of Active Web pages (see Lesson 17, "Active Web Pages with Java and ActiveX") seems to have gotten the most attention, HTML style sheets may turn out to be the most important aspect of the new standard. Accordingly, the subject of style sheets is being introduced early in this *10 Minute Guide*, even before some of the most elementary HTML features.

Many of the features of HTML you'll be learning in this book can be controlled with style sheets under the HTML 4.0 standard. Tedious hand-editing (and re-editing) of a wide variety of older HTML tags can now be avoided through the application of general rules you define in style sheets. Style sheets control text formatting, colors, image placement, and a host of other matters in HTML documents.

Style sheets are easy to define, and can be applied across the board to all your HTML documents, enabling you to present a consistent look in all your Web pages. Moreover, changing the look of your style-sheet-controlled documents is as easy as changing your style sheets; your changes are applied to *all* of your pages at once.

In the lessons that follow, you'll learn not only about individual HTML tags that control these matters, but also about how you can accomplish the same ends using style sheets. While there will no doubt be instances when using style sheets don't meet your needs in setting up your Web pages, as a rule, this book recommends the use of style sheets wherever possible. You'll even learn style sheet workarounds that let you make your HTML documents work, even in browsers that don't support them.

STYLE SHEET BASICS

Every newspaper, magazine, and book publisher uses a written set of rules for its writers, editors, and printers called a **style sheet**. A style sheet governs spelling, punctuation, hyphenation, grammar, usage, style, and other aspects of a written publication. This is why the daily baseball standings or Op-Ed Page in your daily newspaper always look the same from day to day. Similarly, since the English rendering of non-Western proper names often varies, a publication will use a style sheet rule dictating a particular spelling of, say, the President of an Islamic nation; following the rule, the same spelling is always used in that publication.

Authors must follow a set of style sheet rules for the *10 Minute Guide* series of books, like this one, for example, which governs:

- The formatting of the pages;
- Use and size of headings;
- Typefaces used;
- How Que Publishing spells and capitalizes words; and
- Many other similar things.

Applying these rules allows all the books in the *10 Minute Guide* series to have both a common look and a common set of usage, spelling, and punctuation. Your hometown newspaper, favorite magazine, and every book publisher all have style sheets. While they may differ from each other, their use ensures that the day-to-day, month-to-month, or book-to-book look of the publication is consistent and meets professional standards.

HTML STYLE SHEETS

As you've probably guessed by now, HTML style sheets allow you to gain the same sort of overall control of your HTML documents. You can adopt and apply rules about headlines, type size and type face, colors on your Web pages, and a large number of other matters with style sheets. Through their application, your Web pages can take on a consistent, professional look that meets your standards.

Moreover, when you use HTML style sheets, it becomes easier to change the overall look of your Web pages—all of them. Simple changes in your style sheets get automatically propagated to all the HTML documents they control.

Style Sheets Subject to the Hardware   Users running non-graphical, Web browsers like Lynx, or using mono-chrome monitors, may not benefit from all the rules in your style sheets. Of course, the reasons for this are the same as those you learned about in Lesson 1, "Overview of HTML."

KINDS OF STYLE SHEETS

We'll get our fingers dirty with actual HTML markup for style sheets in later lessons. First, though, let's take an overall look at three different kinds of style sheet usage:

- You can apply *in-line* (*ad hoc*) style changes to individual HTML tags within a Web page, changing, say, the point size of just one particular headline or the margins or text color of just one particular paragraph.

- You can *embed* (include) an overall style sheet for an HTML page right in the document itself, allowing you to specify overall formatting and layout of that particular document.

- You can *link* (reference) a general style sheet into multiple HTML documents, enabling use of a single style sheet that applies to all your Web pages. Changing the general style sheet applies the new styles to all your documents.

This will all begin to make more sense to you as you go through the following lessons. The main thing you need to remember from this lesson is that style sheets are very important in HTML 4.0; the time you spend learning about them will pay dividends, making your life as an HTML author easier. As you work your way through the rest of the lessons, you'll learn how use of style sheets fits in with many HTML specifics, like headlines, text fonts, colors, and the like.

Toward the end of this *10 Minute Guide* (Lesson 19, "Cascading Style Sheets"), we'll return to style sheets in more depth. In that lesson, you'll learn about **cascading style sheets**, an unfortunate term that's being thrown around—and misunderstood—a good deal lately. For now, just think of cascading style sheets as being a set of rules for using HTML style sheets, *a style sheet for style sheets*, if you will.

BROWSER SUPPORT FOR **HTML 4.0** STYLE SHEETS

Except for Internet Explorer version 3, most older Web browsers don't support style sheets; IE Version 3 supported HTML version 3.2 style sheets, as well as proprietary Microsoft extensions. Netscape version 3, for example, does not support style sheets at all.

Netscape Communicator's Version 4.x browser has incorporated many HTML 3.2 style sheet features, as well as new, Netscape-proprietary ones. Netscape's new **Dynamic HTML** (DHTML) uses a style-sheet-like mechanism, for instance; see Lesson 20, "Introducing Dynamic HTML." At the time this book was being written, Netscape Communications Corporation had announced support for HTML 4.0 (including style sheets) in an unspecified future release of its Web browser.

Microsoft Internet Explorer version 4 purports to support all HTML 4.0 requirements.

In view of differing (and changing) support for HTML style sheets, what are you as an HTML author to do about them, then? Your best bet is to know which browsers are used by the people who'll be viewing your Web pages. This knowledge will take a major role in your deciding which HTML features to use in your Web pages, including, of course, style sheets.

In this lesson, you've been introduced to HTML 4.0 style sheets, an important foundation for the HTML know-how you'll gain in the remaining lessons. The next lesson turns to some fundamental HTML building blocks, headlines, typeface styles, and paragraphs.

CREATING HEADLINES, TYPEFACE STYLE, AND PARAGRAPHS

In this lesson, you learn to create headlines, type styles, and paragraph tags in your HTML documents, as well as how to use text colors. You'll also see how these aspects of your documents can be controlled using style sheets.

CREATING HEADLINES

You can create headlines of various sizes in your HTML documents using headline tags.

HEADLINE BASICS

HTML supports six levels of headlines, using the tags **<H1>** through **<H6>**; the lower the number, the larger the headline. An HTML headline is very simple:

> **<H1>This is a Level-One (The Largest) Headline</H1>**

Just surround the headline text with start and stop headline tags.

For smaller headline type sizes, use a *larger* number (for example, <H2> or <H5>). Headlines create an **automatic line break** in your documents (see the "Other Line Breaks" section for more on line breaks), and can wrap over multiple lines. You should note the smaller headline sizes—<H3>-<H6>—are rendered on most Web browsers in a type size that's actually *smaller* than regular text. See Figure 6.1 for a sample of <H1> through <H6> headlines.

```
┌──────────────────────────────────────────────────────────────┐
│ ▭                  NCSA Mosaic: Document View              ▫ ▢ │
├──────────────────────────────────────────────────────────────┤
│  File   Options   Navigate   Annotate                   Help │
│                                                              │
│  Title: │ Local file /users/tkevans/headlines.html │   ┌──┐ │
│                                                      │  ◯  │ │
│  URL:   │ file://localhost/users/tkevans/headlines.html │ └──┘ │
│  ┌────────────────────────────────────────────────────────┐  │
│  │                                                        │  │
│  │  Level 1 Headline                                      │  │
│  │                                                        │  │
│  │  Level 2 Headline                                      │  │
│  │                                                        │  │
│  │  Level 3 Headline                                      │  │
│  │                                                        │  │
│  │  Level 4 Headline                                      │  │
│  │                                                        │  │
│  │  Level 5 Headline                                      │  │
│  │                                                        │  │
│  │  Level 6 Headline                                      │  │
│  │                                                        │  │
│  │                                                        │  │
│  └────────────────────────────────────────────────────────┘  │
│                                                              │
│ ┌────┬─────────┬────┬──────┬─────┬─────────┬─────┬──────────┬──────────────┐ │
│ │Back│Forward│Home│Reload│Open...│Save As...│Clone│New Window│Close Window│ │
│ └────┴─────────┴────┴──────┴─────┴─────────┴─────┴──────────┴──────────────┘ │
└──────────────────────────────────────────────────────────────┘
```

FIGURE 6.1 HTML headlines.

HEADLINES AND STYLE SHEETS

Headlines are one of many HTML aspects that can be controlled using style sheets, to which you were introduced in Lesson 5, "Introduction to HTML Style Sheets." Generally, style sheets give you more flexibility in the layout of your Web pages, so you'll want to use them whenever you can. For example, using an **embedded style sheet**, you can alter the font size and style of *all the headlines in a document*, with just one piece of markup.

Embedded Style Sheet Embedded style sheets apply your HTML style preferences across the board in a single HTML document.

Using an embedded style sheet, for instance, you can set all level-1 headlines to be rendered in 18-point italic. Here's the markup to do so:

> **<HTML><HEAD><TITLE>Embedded Style Sheet</TITLE></HEAD>**
>
> **<STYLE TYPE="text/css">**
>
> **H1 { font-size: 18pt; font-style: italic } </STYLE><BODY>**

This looks a bit complex, so let's take it apart.

- First, notice the **<STYLE>** markup for an embedded style sheet occurs within the <HEAD> portion of your document, as you'd expect, since it controls the entire document.

- The **TYPE="text/css" attribute** specifies you're using the standard HTML 4.0 style sheet mechanism, called Cascading Style Sheets (css). For now, consider this as just a piece of HTML boilerplate.

- Your headline specification includes two pairs of instructions, separated by a semicolon, calling for 18-point font-**size** and italic font-**style**. The specification is enclosed in curly braces, { and }.

- Finally, your style definition ends with the usual closing tag </STYLE>.

Attributes   HTML attributes specify characteristics that apply to HTML tags, sort of like adverbs modifying verbs. Thus, the **TYPE** attribute for <STYLE> defines the cascading style sheet mechanism to be used within the document. You'll see more HTML attributes as we go along.

CONTROLLING TYPE STYLES AND CHARACTER FORMATTING

You have some control in HTML over type styles/character formatting matters, like boldfacing and emphasized text. Later in this lesson, you'll also learn about controlling text colors. Style sheets extend this control.

Here is a list of some HTML typeface/character formatting tags, called **phrasal** elements. As usual, all tags require closing tags (<STRONG> requires </STRONG>, and so on).

MEANING	TAG
Bold/Emphasis	<STRONG>
Italic	<EM>
Fixed Type	<CODE>
Citation	<CITE>
Definition	<DFN>

FORMATTING PARAGRAPHS

Paragraphing in HTML takes a bit of getting used to. As we've said, the different Web browsers, running on different computers with different graphical capabilities render documents differently. For one thing, they pretty much decide for themselves how to wrap lines of text in a displayed HTML document, and the end-of-line characters you may have put into an HTML document will likely be ignored. Similarly, while you may include blank lines in your HTML source document, intending them to mark paragraph endings, the user's browser ignores them. *You must explicitly mark paragraphs.*

The paragraph tag in HTML is **<P>** and it goes at the beginning of a new paragraph, except where there is some other line break. (Multiple <P> tags are ignored, so you can't use them to add extra blank lines.) Here is an HTML fragment showing use of the paragraph tag:

> **<HTML><HEAD><TITLE>Paragraphing</TITLE></HEAD>**
>
> **<BODY>Here is some text.**
>
> **<P>Here is a new paragraph</P></BODY></HTML>**

TIP

Closing Tag—</P>   This is *optional*, since a beginning-of-paragraph tag is always a logical end-of-paragraph tag. Any HTML tag that creates a line break, such as a headline, results in the text immediately following the line break to be a new paragraph, so the </P> tag isn't needed in these cases, either.

OTHER LINE BREAKS

Since the paragraph tag causes a blank line to be displayed in a Web browser's rendering of your document, you also need a way to cause a line break to occur *without* an attending blank line. The **
 (line break)** tag does this for you. Here's an HTML fragment showing its use, as well as clarifying the difference between it and the <P> tag:

For more information, contact:

> **<P>John Doe
**
>
> **123 Main Street
**
>
> **Htmltown, USA 55555**
>
> **<P>Resumption of document text...**

When rendered, this is displayed with a blank line before "John Doe," but with line breaks (no blank line) between the lines of the address, and a new paragraph (preceded by a blank line) after the

Zip Code line (See Figure 6.2). You can use multiple <BR> tags to force multiple blank lines in your document.

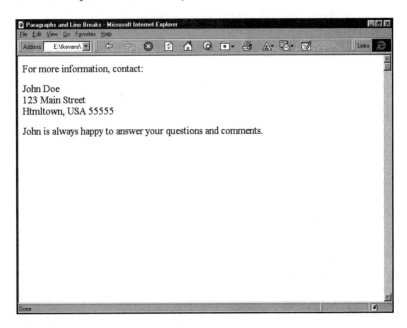

FIGURE 6.2   Paragraphs and line breaks.

Be aware several other HTML tags, by definition, always create line breaks. As noted previously, headlines always break the text and start a new line. Similarly, **lists** (see Lesson 9, "Creating Lists"), **tables** (see Lesson 10, "Creating Tables"), and some of the **logical formatting tags** create line breaks. In these cases, you don't need to include line-break (or paragraph) tags.

> **Suppressing Line Break**   Netscape version 3 supported nonstandard tags for suppressing line breaks and "suggesting" places for line breaks. HTML 4.0 supports "soft" spaces and hyphens which allow for lines to be broken at suggested places, if needed.

TEXT COLORS

You can specify the color of text in your HTML documents. There is a list of 16 simple colors that are supported by name in HTML 4.0:

black	silver
gray	white
maroon	red
purple	fuchsia
green	lime
olive	yellow
navy	blue
teal	aqua

One way you can specify text color is to use an **in-line** style sheet. In-line style sheets set styles for *parts* of HTML documents, while, as you learned earlier in this lesson, embedded style sheets apply to a document as a whole. Suppose you'd like a single paragraph of your document to appear in a different color text than the rest. Here's an HTML fragment using an in-line style sheet to do this:

> **...standard text in your document</P>**
>
> **<P STYLE="color: blue">This paragraph will appear in blue text.</P>**
>
> **<p>...document resumes in normal text color**

As you can see, the STYLE attribute comes within the <P> tag, and applies only to the text up to the next paragraph tag.

If these 16 colors don't meet your needs, there's a means of getting almost any color. This mechanism is based on the notation of colors by using the mix of red, green, and blue colors (RGB). Individual colors are specified by setting each of the three RGB values between 0 and 255. Royal blue, for instance, is expressed as "65 105 225."

Mixing Style Sheets   You're probably wondering whether you can mix embedded and in-line style sheets in the same HTML page, and, if so, what happens. The short answer is "Yes," but hold this thought until Lesson 19, "Cascading Style Sheets," where you'll learn about style sheet precedence.

To set text colors in HTML, grab your scientific calculator (or pop up your Windows calculator in scientific mode) and convert your three decimal color numbers into **hexadecimal (base 16)**. You can also use the Windows 95 Paint program to select colors and display their hex equivalents. To change the text color in the preceding example from blue to royal blue, replace **color: blue** with **color: 4169E1.**

Colors, Colors, and More Colors   Simple arithmetic indicates there's a vast range of possible combinations of these color designations. It's a lot easier to choose colors if you can see them. To do just that, check out **http://www.onr.com/user/lights/colclick.html, http://www.reednews.co.uk/colours.html,** or **http://alberti.crs4.it/colori/f108.html.** Also, UNIX systems generally have a list of colors and their decimal number equivalents in the file /usr/lib/X11/rgb.txt (/usr/openwin/lib/rgb.txt on Sun systems). This is a plain-text file you can read.

This lesson covered fundamental typeface/character formatting issues, highlighting the difference between logical and physical typeface formatting, along with paragraphs and other line breaks, and text colors. You also learned how to use style sheets to control headlines and colors. In the next lesson, you'll learn about Uniform Resource Locators, which help allow you to specify locations on the World Wide Web.

CREATING DOCUMENTS WITH URLs

*In this lesson, you learn about
Uniform Resource Locators, or URLs, the pointers in HTML documents
that lead to various services on the World Wide Web.*

WHAT IS A UNIFORM RESOURCE LOCATOR?

The Uniform Resource Locator, or URL, is the key to locating and interpreting information on the World Wide Web. URLs are a standard way of describing both the location of a Web resource and its content. URLs in HTML documents help you locate Web resources, regardless of whether it's another document on your local computer or on another computer halfway around the world. To create HTML documents with hyperlinks in them, you need to understand the basics of URLs.

> **Hyperlinks** The colored words and phrases you've seen in Web documents are hyperlinks. Clicking them lets you jump to the location pointed to by the link.

All URLs follow a standard format. It looks like this:

servicename://internethost:portnumber/resource

As you can see, there are three parts to this syntax:

- **Service Name** is followed by a colon and two forward slashes (there are a couple of exceptions to the requirement for the slashes, as we'll see later).

- **Internet hostname**, followed by an optional colon and **port number**, followed by a single forward slash.

- **Resource** is normally a document or file on the computer, but it may also be other kinds of resources, as we'll see.

Connections Internet services use imaginary wires to connect services between imaginary plugs (ports) on two computers. These virtual connections are managed by the network software using an abstraction called port numbers. Except where you need to include one in an URL, you really don't need to know anything more than how to recognize one in an URL.

Here's an example URL, showing the required parts:

http://www.yourcompany.com/home.html

CREATING AN URL

1. Identify the service name you will include in your URL. The most commonly used one is the **http** service.

HyperText Transfer Protocol (http) The way Web servers and clients communicate over the network.

2. Identify the **Internet location** of the resource. This is an Internet hostname, such as **ww.yourcompany.com**.

3. Identify the name of the resource, such as a document name, file name, or other resource. An example might be **home.html**.

Using the examples in the preceding listing, we can construct an URL that might represent your company's home page:

http://www.yourcompany.com/index.html

> **TIP**
> **No Name** Web servers and browsers will look for the file named *index.html* if you don't specify a full URL, so the precediing can be shortened to **http://www. yourcompany.com/**.

EXAMPLES OF DIFFERENT SERVICE URLs

This section provides example URLs covering some of the major URL types. Each example is an actual World Wide Web resource that you can access using your Web browser. This is not a complete list of URL types.

THE HTTP URL

The **http URL** represents a document available from a World Wide Web server. Here is an example, the World Wide Web Consortium's Home Page, in fact:

http://www.w3.org/

> **TIP**
> **What Is That Forward Slash?** All URLs use the **forward slash (/)** to specify documents. Even if you're setting up your Web server on a PC, use the forward slash in your URLs, not the **backslash (\)**, to specify the path to a file or document.

Figure 7.1 shows the above http URL example. Notice the URL displayed in the **Location** box near the top of the figure.

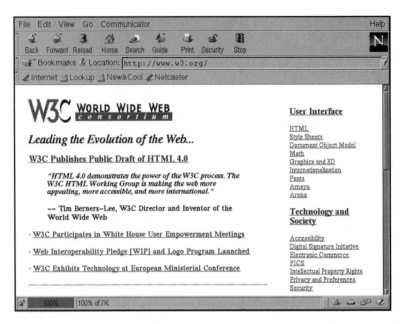

FIGURE 7.1 The http URL.

Secure http You may encounter URLs of the *https* type (note the added "s"). These are secure http URLs, which operate using the Netscape **Secure Sockets Layer** (SSL) protocol to ensure the authenticity of the documents. You can look up SSL at **http://developer.netscape.com/**.

THE FTP URL

This represents the Internet file transfer protocol service. An Internet service that predated the World Wide Web, ftp allows you to transfer documents between remote computers and your own. Here is an example:

ftp://gatekeeper.dec.com/pub/

Note here we have not specified a file name, but rather a directory name (pub/). ftp URLs can also specify file names. This URL is an archive of no-cost software maintained by the Digital Equipment Corporation for customers and others; it's freely accessible.

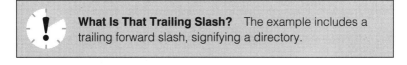

What Is That Trailing Slash?   The example includes a trailing forward slash, signifying a directory.

Figure 7.2 shows a directory listing from this ftp site. As you can see, it's shown pretty much all in text, but notice all the folders shown are hyperlink. Selecting one takes you to that folder; clicking a file name within a folder downloads that file to your computer.

```
FTP directory /pub/ at gatekeeper.dec.com - Microsoft Internet Explorer
File  Edit  View  Go  Favorites  Help
Address ftp://gatekeeper                                                    Links

FTP directory /pub/ at gatekeeper.dec.com

Up to higher level directory

04/14/95 12:00AM         Directory Alpha
06/17/96 12:00AM         Directory BSD
05/01/97 02:00PM         Directory DEC
04/14/95 12:00AM                 3 Digital
08/04/97 02:30PM         Directory GNU
04/14/95 12:00AM         Directory Mach
04/14/95 12:00AM         Directory NIST
07/11/95 12:00AM         Directory UCB
04/18/97 01:31PM         Directory VMS
01/05/97 12:00AM         Directory X11
04/14/95 12:00AM         Directory X11-contrib
04/14/95 12:00AM         Directory athena
04/14/95 12:00AM         Directory case
04/14/95 12:00AM         Directory comm
04/14/95 12:00AM         Directory conferences
04/14/95 12:00AM         Directory data
04/14/95 12:00AM         Directory database
06/28/97 05:17PM         Directory dcpi

Done
```

FIGURE 7.2   The ftp URL.

THE NEWS URL

The News URL represents the Usenet news service. **Usenet**, often called **netnews**, is a vastly distributed bulletin board service (BBS), organized into tens of thousands of special interest subject areas. Usenet, too, is an Internet service that existed before the Web and which was folded into it. An example news URL is:

news:comp.infosystems.www.authoring.html

Figure 7.3 shows an example listing. This example is a newsgroup dedicated to the discussion of HTML authoring. As you'll note, there's a scrollable list of news "articles" in the upper pane of the main window. Clicking an article opens its text in the lower pane. While this screenshot shows Netscape, you'll find other browsers present Usenet news in a similar way. Using your Web browser, you can not only read Usenet news articles, but also reply to them with either e-mail or a follow-up article of your own. In addition, you can post your own articles.

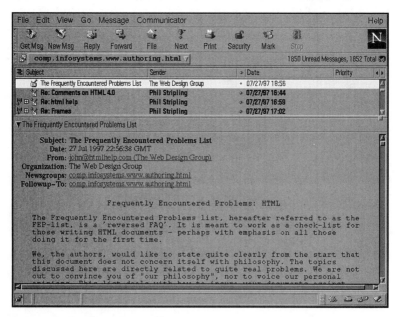

FIGURE 7.3 The news URL.

> **Where Are the Forward Slashes?** The news URL is an
> exception to the rule requiring the two forward slashes in
> the first of the three parts of the URL; only the colon and
> the newsgroup name are required.

THE MAILTO URL

This represents the Internet electronic mail (e-mail) service.
The mailto URL is supported by most Web browsers. If you include mailto URL in your HTML documents, readers can send
you e-mail simply by clicking the hyperlink. Here is an example:

mailto:webmaster@www.yourcompany.com

Notice the e-mail address in Figure 7.3 (the line beginning with
"From:"), which was generated with a mailto URL. Netscape's
Collabra UseNet news reader (part of the overall Netscape Communicator package) automatically extracts the e-mail address of
an article's poster and creates the mailto URL when it displays the
article. If you post UseNet news articles, your e-mail address will
appear in them as mailto URLs.

> **Spam** Lately, nearly everyone with an e-mail account
> has been hit by junk e-mail, often called **spam**. Usenet is
> one place spam marketers get e-mail addresses.

THE FILE URL

This represents a file located on your own computer. Here is an
example:

file://winword6/html/myfile.htm

> **Where's the Last "l" in That URL?**   Older versions of
> DOS allow only three characters in a file name extension,
> whereas other systems, such as UNIX systems or Win-
> dows 95/NT, allow more. This URL refers to a file on an
> older PC.

You'll recall using a file URL in Lesson 4, "Creating a Simple HTML Document," to view your first HTML page in your Web browser. As you saw, the file URL is an important one; it allows you to see what your pages look like, make changes, correct errors, and so on, before you make them available on the Web.

Some HTML authors mistakenly use the file URL interchangeably with the ftp URL. This can lead to problems, so always use the correct URL type.

OTHER URL TYPES

There are several other, less commonly used, URL types. These include the **WAIS** (Wide Area Indexing Servers) URL, for doing keyword searches in WAIS databases on the Web; **gopher**, a text-based menu-oriented predecessor to the World Wide Web; and others. WAIS keyword support has been for the most part supplanted by other Web services called Search Engines, while gopher services are becoming more and more rare. A large number of other URL types have been proposed, though not all are supported by current Web browsers. You can read about them, including viewing a more or less official list, on the Web at **http:// www.w3.org/Addressing/schemes.html**.

This lesson has covered Uniform Resource Locators: what they look like and how they are formatted. We've seen the various kinds of URLs and the Internet services they represent. In the next lesson, you learn how to use URLs to make hyperlinks in your HTML documents.

USING
ANCHORS AND
LINKS

*In this lesson, you learn to use tags
and URLs to create hyperlinks to local and remote documents and
services on the Web.*

WHAT IS A HYPERLINK?

You've used hyperlinks as you've tooled around the World Wide
Web. Your knowledge of URLs and just the few HTML tags you've
learned so far is the basis for this lesson. The new **anchor** tag,
introduced in this lesson, completes this picture.

Click and Go Hyperlinks are the colored/highlighted
words and phrases you see in Web documents. When
you click them, you jump to other documents on the local
Web server or documents or services somewhere out on
the Internet, across town or halfway around the world.

THE ANCHOR HTML TAG

Hyperlinks are based on the **anchor** HTML tag. Like all HTML
tags, this one requires opening and closing pairs. Here is the general format:

<A COMMAND="target">Highlighted Text</A>

Let's take this apart and look at it, piece by piece. First, the matter inside the first pair of brackets, **<A COMMAND="target">**:

- As with other HTML attributes, there are two parts here, separated by the = sign. The right side is shown inside double quotation marks (this isn't a strict requirement in all situations, but it's a good idea to follow it anyway, especially if it contains spaces).

- On the left, you'll use either the **HREF** or **NAME** attributes, replacing COMMAND. HREF signifies a hyperlink, whereas NAME signifies a marked placed in the document (we'll focus on HREF here, then cover NAME a little later).

- The right side of the = sign is the *destination* of the hyperlink. As you already learned, the destination can be a document on your own computer, or a document or service out on the Internet.

Let's now turn to the part of the anchor we've labeled **Highlighted Text</A>** in our example:

- Before you can select a hyperlink in a Web document, you must be able to see some **highlighted text** connected to the hyperlink. It's this part of the anchor tag that specifies the word or phrase to appear as highlighted in the HTML document.

- The closing **</A>** at the end of your anchor is required. When the HTML document is displayed, the words *Highlighted Text* are highlighted.

> **TIP**
>
> **Assemble the Link**   Putting the anchor link together, including the material on both sides of the "=" sign, is what produces your highlighted hyperlink.

LINKING TO LOCAL DOCUMENTS

The simplest hyperlink is one pointing to another document on the same computer. Let's say you have two HTML documents named *doc1.htm* and *doc2.htm*. To jump from the first to the second document, add an anchor in doc1.htm like this:

<A HREF="doc2.htm">Highlighted Text to Appear</A>

Following is a very simple, complete HTML document illustrating an anchor tag pointing to a local document (that is, a file on your own computer).

<HTML><HEAD>

<TITLE>Simple HTML Doc with Local Link</TITLE>

</HEAD><BODY>

<H1>HTML document with a Hyperlink to a Local File</H1>

Welcome to my Web page.

<P>Please try out <A HREF="doc2.htm">my first hyperlink</A>

</BODY></HTML>

> **Where's the Link?** If you've typed in this example document and tried it out, you probably got an error message. This is because the target document, named *doc2.htm* in this example, hasn't been created yet.

Figures 8.1 shows what this document looks like in a Web browser. Clicking the hyperlink (the phrase "my first hyperlink") opens the new document.

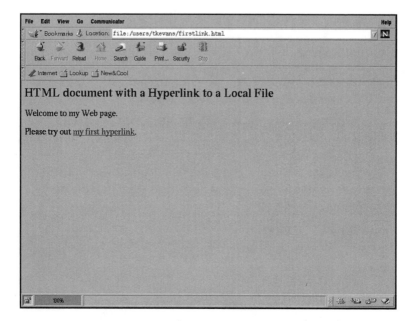

FIGURE 8.1   Simple HTML document with link to local file.

What If the Target Document Is in a Different Directory?   The example assumes both documents are in the same directory, or folder. If you need to reference a document in a different directory, simply change the target part of the anchor tag to include the directory path. For example, if *doc2.htm* is in the subdirectory *subdir1*, your anchor would read:

<A HREF="subdir1/doc2.htm">

Note the use of the **forward slash**, not the backslash you might be used to. You can, of course, use a full directory path, such as *C:/myfiles/subdir1/doc2.htm* or a relative path, such as *../subdir1/doc2.htm*, depending on how you've organized your directories and subdirectories.

LINKING TO SPECIFIC PLACES IN A DOCUMENT

Now that you know how to link to another document, you may want your hyperlink to point to a specific spot in the target document, instead of just to the document itself. For example, you might have a table-of-contents document with hyperlinks to each section of the main document listed. This is easy in HTML. Recall the format of anchors, **<A COMMAND="target">Highlighted Text</A>**. Here, instead of HREF, you'll use the NAME attribute. The syntax is simple:

<A NAME="something">

The NAME anchor is a just a *marker*. It goes in your *target* document at the spot you want the hyperlink in the first document to take the reader. For example, here's an HTML fragment from a target document with a marked spot:

<A NAME="chap3">

Moving back to your first document, you can use an anchor to create a hyperlink to this spot in your target document:

You'll find additional information <A HREF="doc2.htm#chap3">Chapter 3</A>

As you can see, this is a normal hyperlink to a local document, but with one difference: the addition of "#chap3" to reference the spot you've marked in the target document. Clicking the hyperlink in your first document jumps you not only to the target document, but also right to the marked spot in it. You can fine-tune your HTML documents by enabling users to jump to a precise spot.

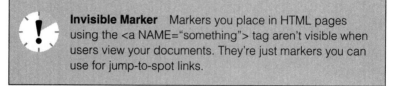

Invisible Marker   Markers you place in HTML pages using the <a NAME="something"> tag aren't visible when users view your documents. They're just markers you can use for jump-to-spot links.

Incidentally, you can also use the jump-to-a-spot feature within a single document. Just place your marker and then create your hyperlink in the same document, like this:

<A HREF="#spot">Highlighted Text</A>

Here's an HTML fragment, showing this feature within the same document.

This page provides access to an assortment of tools and information for WebMasters (people who run WWW servers or who create hypertext markup language (HTML) documents for WWW servers).

<P>From this page, you can

[Some text deleted]

<LI>Learn about the <A HREF="#htmlrefs">Hyper Text Markup Language</A></LI>

[Some text deleted]

<A NAME="htmlrefs"><H2>Hyper Text Markup Language (HTML)</H2></A>

Figure 8.2 shows the page from which this fragment is taken. There's a list of hyperlinks; our fragment is the fourth item on that list.

As you can see, this is a full hyperlink, with "#htmlrefs" as its target. The last line of the preceding HTML source fragment is the target of this hyperlink. You'll note the use of the "<A NAME="htmlrefs">." Selecting the hyperlink jumps you to the destination spot within the same document, as shown in Figure

8.3. Note the appearance of the "#htmlrefs" in Netscape's Location box.

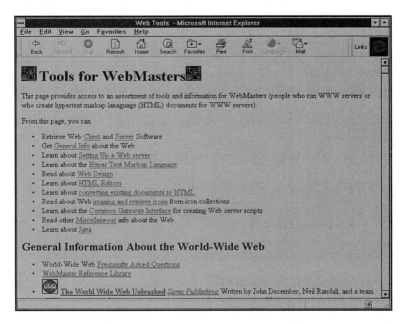

FIGURE 8.2   HTML document with jump-to-spot links.

LINKING URLs

We can now turn to the main objective of this lesson: links that point to documents or other resources on remote systems. To do this, we'll use the **Uniform Resource Locators** you learned in the last lesson. Let's look back at the first URL example we discussed:

http://www.w3.org/

Creating a hyperlink containing this URL is pretty straightforward, using what we've learned about anchors:

<A HREF="http://www.w3.org">World Wide Web Consortium</A> Home Page

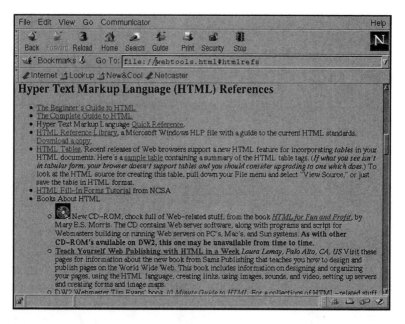

FIGURE 8.3   Destination document.

As you can see, we've simply dropped the complete URL into the *target* slot (to the right of the = sign) in our anchor tag. In HTML terms, the URL is part of the HREF attribute.

The phrase *World Wide Web Consortium* is highlighted, and you can jump to it with just a click of your mouse.

Other URLs work exactly the same way in anchors. Here's the second example we used in Lesson 7, the DEC anonymous ftp server:

<A HREF="ftp://gatekeeper.dec.com/pub/">Digital Equipment Corp's</A> Anonymous ftp Server

The following is a complete HTML document containing links to all the URL examples in Lesson 7. A Netscape rendering of that HTML document is shown in Figure 8.4.

```
<HTML><HEAD><TITLE>Example URL's from Les-
son 7</TITLE></HEAD><BODY><H1>Example URL's
from Lesson 7</H1>
```

This lists the example URL's from Lesson 7, each one
of which is a clickable hyperlink.

```
<H2><A HREF="http://www.w3.org">World Wide
Web Consortium</A> Home Page</H2>
```

```
<H2><A HREF="ftp://gatekeeper.dec.com/
pub">Digital Equipment Corporation's</A>
Anonymous ftp Server</H2>
```

```
<H2><A
HREF="news:comp.infosystems.www.authoring.html">
comp.infosystems.www.authoring.html</A>
USENET news group</H2>
```

```
<H2>Send E-Mail to our <A HREF="mailto:
webmaster@www.yourcompany.com">Webmaster
</A></H2>
```

```
<H2><A HREF="file://winword6/html/
myfile.htm">Local File</A> on My Computer</H2>
```

```
</BODY></HTML>
```

TIP   **Links Inside Other Markup**   Notice our hyperlinks are
embedded right in the Level-2 (<H2>) headlines, illustrating how HTML markup allows you a great deal of flexibility. (Note also the use of multiple headlines to create a
kind of list; you'll learn true HTML markup for lists in Lesson 9, "Creating Lists.")

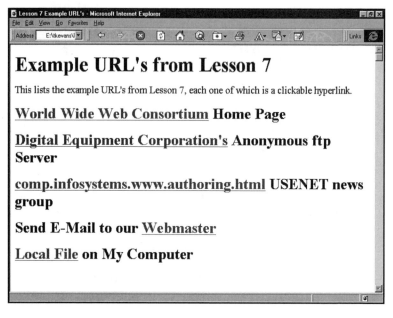

FIGURE 8.4   Hyperlinks to Lesson 7 sample URLs.

Absolute and Relative URLs   By now, you've figured out hyperlinks to local documents are actually little URLs, but without the service name and Internet host name. When referring to documents that use the same service name and host name as the parent document, you can use **relative** URLs. Using relative URLs allows you to move whole HTML document trees from one place to another, even to another computer, without having to go back through all the documents and change the absolute URLs.

In this lesson, you've learned to create hyperlinks in your HTML documents by using Uniform Resource Locators. We'll return to HTML formatting and layout in the next lesson, as we turn to adding lists to your HTML documents.

CREATING LISTS

In this lesson, you learn how to format several kinds of HTML lists.

KINDS OF LISTS

It's useful to have your HTML documents contain formatted lists of items, in addition to ordinary paragraphs of text. HTML supports several different list formats, each with enough variations to give you a wide range of capabilities. These include:

- Bulleted lists, called **unordered** lists in HTML
- Sequentially numbered/lettered lists, called **ordered** lists
- Glossary lists

HTML has markup tags for each of these kinds of lists.

FORMATTING BULLETS (UNORDERED LISTS)

Bulleted lists highlight each item on a list by adding a typographical bullet or other distinctive marker. In HTML, bullets are created automatically when you use the unordered list markup tag, **<UL>**, together with the generic **<LI>, list item** tag. Here is an HTML fragment containing an unordered list:

<UL><LI>First Bulleted Item</LI>

<LI>Second Bulleted Item</LI>

<LI>Last Bulleted Item</LI></UL>

By now, you're familiar enough with HTML markup syntax to recognize the start and stop <UL> markers for the overall list, as well as the markers for the individual items <LI>.

> **TIP**
>
> **I Before E, Except After C**   While the list-close marker </UL> is always required, the HTML 4.0 standard doesn't require the closing </LI> tag, and most current Web browsers just ignore them. Nonetheless, rather than learning exceptions to general HTML rules, it's a good idea to just go ahead and use the list item close marker. Doing so provides a visual clue that makes it easier for you to proofread your HTML code.

Figure 9.1 shows an unordered list, as well as an ordered list (see next section). List items need not be confined to a single line of text. You can use several lines of text, creating hanging indents. Also, you can use paragraph markers <P> and </P> to create multi-paragraph, bulleted lists.

> **Mixing Tags**   Be careful when mixing other HTML tags within your lists, however. In particular, note that line-breaking HTML tags, such as the <BR> tag or a headline tag, may have unexpected effects on your lists. When in doubt, use your Web browser's capability to preview your HTML document before putting it on the Web.

> **Hanging Indents**   Bulleted lists produce hanging indents. In other words, the paragraph begins with a bullet, and each line of the paragraph is indented from the left margin, rather than returning to the margin. The whole paragraph "hangs" directly below the bullet.

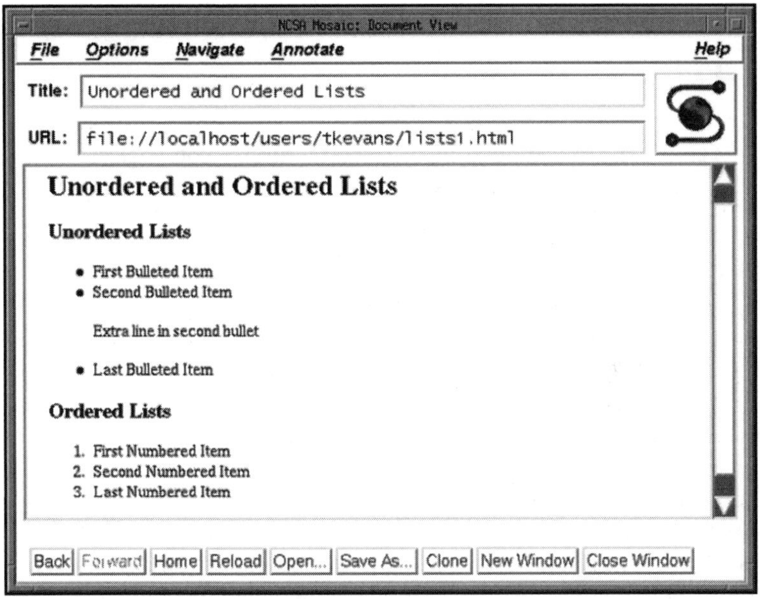

FIGURE 9.1   Unordered and ordered lists.

If you're not happy with the default bullets you get with an unordered list, you have two other choices. Using an HTML unordered list *attribute*, you can select one of two other bullet types, the **square** and **hollow circle** types. Here's an HTML fragment showing the square bullet type.

> **<UL TYPE=SQUARE>**
>
> **<LI>First Item</LI>**
>
> **...**
>
> **</UL>**

As you can see, the attribute **"TYPE=SQUARE"** appears immediately after the open-list tag, within the angle brackets. To use the hollow circle bullet type, use **"TYPE=CIRCLE."** The default bullet type for unordered lists is **"TYPE=DISC"** and is not required. (The difference between CIRCLE and DISC is the former generates a hollow circle, while the latter generates a filled circle.)

FORMATTING NUMBERED (ORDERED) LISTS

Instead of bullets, you may want to have your lists **numbered** or **lettered**. HTML's ordered list tag **<OL>** allows you to do just that—and automatically numbers/letters your items for you. Here's an example HTML fragment:

> **<OL><LI>First Numbered Item</LI>**
>
> **<LI>Second Numbered Item</LI>**
>
> **<LI>Third Numbered Item</LI></OL>**

Note the use of the standard <LI> and </LI> tags for the individual list items. Also, your ordered list is automatically numbered when it's interpreted and displayed by your user's Web browser, so you don't need to type any numbers in your HTML document; it will be renumbered automatically if you add or delete items later. Figure 9.1 shows both an ordered and unordered list as interpreted and displayed.

There is a **TYPE** attribute for ordered lists that allows you to tailor your ordered lists, allowing several kinds of numbering, and selection of letters as well. Use the TYPE attribute just as you did with your unordered list, with one of the following:

TYPE	DEFINITION
1	Arabic Numbers (the default; not required; this is a number one, not the letter "I")
a	Lowercase Letters
A	Uppercase Letters
i	Small Roman Numerals
I	Large Roman Numerals

For example, <OL TYPE="i"> generates an ordered list using small Roman Numerals.

> **Just in Case**   Throughout this book, use of all upper-case characters has been recommended for your HTML markup. Although this remains a good idea, you can see the ordered list numbering types are case-sensitive.

There may be instances when you'd like to control the starting number used in an ordered list. For example, you may need to interrupt a list with some other material, then resume it at the same point. To do so, close your first list, add your intervening material, then start a new list, using the **START** attribute. Here's an example HTML fragment, calling for an ordered list to use large Roman Numerals and to begin numbering with the VII, illustrating use of multiple list attributes at once.

<OL TYPE="I" START="7">

...

</OL>

> **All Gaul Is Divided into III Parts**   You must use an Arabic number (that is, 1, 2, 3, and so on) to define an alternative starting number in a list, even though you may have specified a Roman Numeral or Letter numbering type.

CREATING GLOSSARY LISTS

A glossary listing allows you to include a description of each item listed. The HTML tag **<DL>** denotes such a list, but uses a couple of other tags to format the glossary listing. The others are **<DT>**, *definition term*, and **<DD>**, *definition data*. Here's an example HTML fragment:

<H1>HTML List Elements</H1>

```
<DL><DT>The UL Tag</DT>

<DD>Creates an unordered, or bulleted, list</DD>

<DT>The OL tag</DT>

<DD>Creates an ordered, or numbered list</DD>

<DT>The LI Tag</DT>

<DD>Used in both unordered and ordered lists to
denote list items.</DD>

<DT>The DL Tag</DT>

<DD>Create a glossary or dictionary list</DD>

<DT>The DT Tag</DT>

<DD>Delineates a term on a definition list</DD>

<DT>The DD Tag</DT>

<DD>A definition on a dictionary or glossary list
</DD></DL>
```

Figure 9.2 shows the rendering of this example, and a quick summary of the HTML list tags.

USING IMAGES AS BULLETS

You've probably seen attractive lists on Web pages that use images rather than the plain bullets created with HTML list markup. While you'll learn about images in Lesson 11, "Adding Images to Your Document," take a look at the following HTML fragment, which uses a combination of a glossary list, images, the <em> text-formatting tag, and other HTML markup to create the attractive list shown in Figure 9.3 (the bullets are green).

```
<DL><DT><IMG SRC="greenball.gif"><a

href="http://www.mycompany.com/
discussions">DW2 Group Discussions</A>
```

<DD><EM>Threaded group discussions...</EM><HR>

<DT><IMG SRC="greenball.gif"><a

href="http://www.mycompany.com/ whats_new.html">What's New in DW2</a>

<DD><EM>This branch is frequently updated... </EM><HR>

...

</DL>

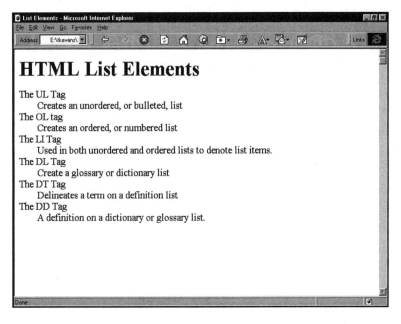

FIGURE 9.2   Glossary list.

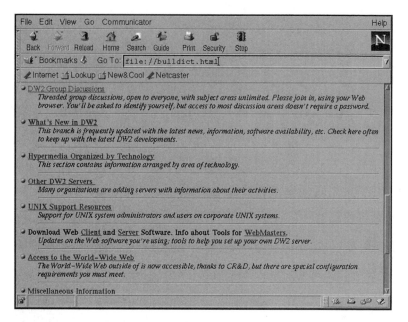

Figure 9.3 A sample bulleted list.

Nesting Lists

You can also nest lists, even different kinds of listings. (A nested list is a list within a list.) For example, the following HTML fragment shows a two-level unordered list:

<UL><LI>List Item Number 1</LI>

<LI>List Item Number 2</LI>

<UL><LI>Item 2 sub-item A</LI>

<LI>Item 2 sub-item B</LI></UL>

<LI>List Item Number 3</LI></UL>

Figure 9.4 shows the nested list created by this example markup. In addition, this figure shows a nested list, using both ordered and unordered list tags; the HTML fragment follows.

<OL><LI>Apples</LI>

<UL><LI>Granny</LI>

<LI>Golden Delicious</LI></UL>

<LI>Oranges</LI>

<UL><LI>Navel</LI>

<LI>Juice</LI></UL></OL>

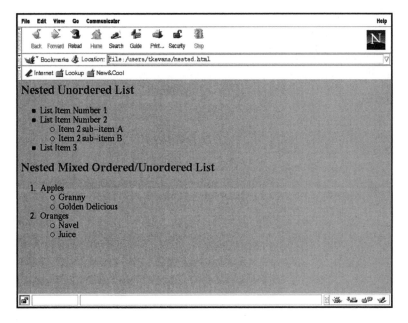

Nested Unordered List

- List Item Number 1
- List Item Number 2
  - Item 2 sub–item A
  - Item 2 sub–item B
- List Item 3

Nested Mixed Ordered/Unordered List

1. Apples
   - Granny
   - Golden Delicious
2. Oranges
   - Navel
   - Juice

FIGURE 9.4   Nested lists.

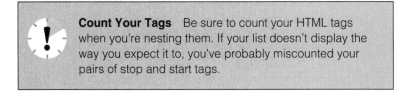

Count Your Tags   Be sure to count your HTML tags when you're nesting them. If your list doesn't display the way you expect it to, you've probably miscounted your pairs of stop and start tags.

This lesson covered the various kinds of lists you can put into
your HTML documents. In addition, you've learned that lists can
be nested to create useful effects. In the next lesson, we'll go into
tables and other specially formatted material.

CREATING TABLES

10

In this lesson, you learn HTML markup for on-screen tables. Tables are used not only for tabular data, like columns of numbers, but also for the creation of striking Web pages.

Even with the improvements in HTML 4.0, different Web browsers, running on different computer hardware, render your HTML in different ways, by using various fonts, breaking lines in different places, and generally precluding you from doing much firm document layout. So, how can you preserve essential layout such as tables in your HTML documents?

> **Table Talk** An HTML table, like any other printed table, consists of columns and rows of information.

The latest HTML standard includes important ways of creating tables, which you can use not only for tabular material, but also to gain more control over the on-screen display of other documents. In fact, many HTML authors find the latter capability more important than mere presentation of tabular data. Use of **HTML tables markup** can control the layout and presentation of images and other material having nothing at all to do with columns and rows of numbers.

TABLE BASICS

Nonetheless, it's best to think of HTML tables as simple **spreadsheets**, such as Lotus 1-2-3 or Excel. Spreadsheets consist of horizontal **rows** and vertical **columns** of information, which can be formatted according to your needs. The intersection of a row and a column is called a **cell**. HTML cells contain either data— numbers, text, an image—or **header information** describing the data in a column or row.

An HTML table won't do math, but if you're experienced with the basics of spreadsheets, you should be on familiar ground here. Because it's the best way to introduce tables, we'll start our tables discussion with simple tabular data and then move into sophisticated use of table markup for images and other data.

USING HEADING, ROW, AND DATA TAGS

HTML uses the **<TABLE> markup** tag to signify a table. An HTML table has three main markup tags: **<TH>** for table heading information; **<TR>** marking a table row; and **<TD>** for table **data** (that is, the information in a cell), as well as several attributes. Here's an HTML fragment with a very simple table:

<TABLE><TR><TD>Row 1, Column 1</TD>

<TD>Row 1, Column 2</TD>

<TR><TD>Row 2, Column 1</TD>

<TD>Row 2, Column 2</TD></TABLE>

This prints a simple two-row, two-column table.

 Vertical and Horizontal Headings Table heading is a bit of a misnomer; it applies both to vertical column headings and horizontal row labels.

Let's modify our previous example fragment to add some real information:

<H1>Consolidated HTML Consultants, Inc.</H1>

<H2>1998 Profit and Loss (Actual and Forecast)</H2>

<TABLE><TR><TH>First Quarter</TH>

<TH>Second Quarter</TH><TH>Third Quarter</TH>

<TH>Fourth Quarter</TH> </TR)

<TR><TD>12% Profit (Actual)</TD>

<TD>2% Loss (Actual)</TD>

<TD>5% Loss (Actual)</TD>

<TD>8% Profit (Actual)</TD>

<TR><TD>11% profit (Forecast)</TD>

<TD>2% profit(Forecast)</TD>

<TD>3% loss (Forecast)</TD>

<TD>5% profit (Forecast)</TD></TABLE>

Here, we added four headings for our quarterly report of profit and loss, and added two rows of actual data, along with a couple of descriptive headlines. Figure 10.1 shows our table.

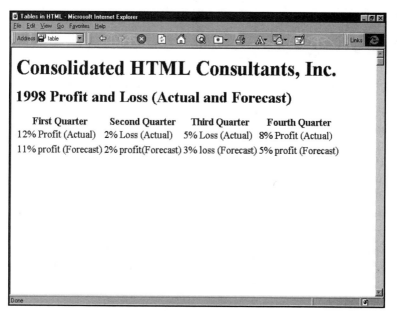

FIGURE 10.1 Table with table headings added.

ADDING ALIGNMENT

One of the first things you'll notice about the table (besides the slightly different, bolded typeface automatically added for the table headings) is the *formatting of the cells*. The contents of each table heading and cell are centered within the cell, which is the default. <TH> and <TD> each support the **ALIGN** attribute, which gives you control over the justification of the contents of a cell. Simply insert the attribute into the markup tag. For example, to use left alignment, use **<TH ALIGN="LEFT">**; for right justification, use **<TD ALIGN="RIGHT">**. As with other HTML attributes, you should surround table attributes with double quotes.

CONTROLLING COLUMNS AND ROWS

There are a couple of additional attributes supported by both <TH> and <TD>. You can control the width and height of columns and rows using the **COLSPAN** and **ROWSPAN** attributes. For example, **<TH ROWSPAN=3>** creates a table heading that is three rows *high*, while **<TD COLSPAN=2>** creates a cell that is two columns *wide*. Imaginative use of the COLSPAN and ROWSPAN attributes allow you to create quite complex tables, as you'll see.

CREATING A COMPLEX, BOXED TABLE

Figure 10.2 shows a complex table, using both the COLSPAN and ROWSPAN attributes. First, notice this table is neatly boxed. It's very simple to box your tables with the **BORDER** attribute of the <TABLE> markup tag, as in **<TABLE BORDER>**. <CAPTION> is an HTML tag you can use to add a title to your tables. Like <TD> and <TR>, <CAPTION> is valid only within a <TABLE> tag and can specify your table title like this:

<CAPTION>Title of the Table</CAPTION>

Here's some of the HTML markup for the table in Figure 10.2. The full listing is too long to reproduce, and it contains much repetition. We've omitted much of the repetition to shorten it.

<TABLE BORDER ALIGN=BLEEDRIGHT>

<TR><TH ALIGN="LEFT">Tag</TH>

<TH>Attributes</TH>

<TH COLSPAN=25 ALIGN="RIGHT">What it Means</TH>

<TR><TD ALIGN=LEFT><TABLE></TD>

<TD>None</TD>

<TD COLSPAN=25 ALIGN=RIGHT>Signifies this is a table</TD>

<TR><TD ALIGN=LEFT><TR></TD>

<TD>None</TD>

<TD COLSPAN=25 ALIGN="RIGHT">End of Table Row</TD>

<TR><TD ROWSPAN=3 ALIGN=LEFT><TH> </TH>

<TR><TD>COLSPAN</TD>

<TD COLSPAN=25 ALIGN="RIGHT">Width in columns</TD>

<TR><TD>ROWSPAN</TD>

<TR><TD>SPAN</TD>

> **<—What?**   Figure 10.2 contains the literal "<" and ">" characters, normally used in HTML markup, and you might wonder how to use these characters in Web pages. The HTML markup that creates this table uses special character strings to produce these figures, **<** and **>**, respectively. Note the leading *ampersand* character and the ending *semicolon*. HTML supports a relatively large number of these **entity references** to represent the full ISO Latin-1 character set. Entity references include symbols, like the circled-C copyright symbol, and special characters, like the *umlaut*, used in non-English languages.

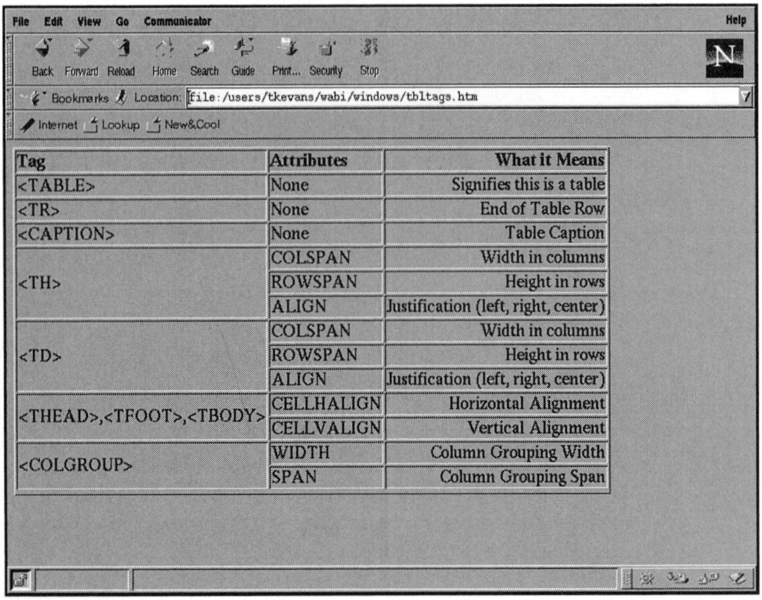

Tag	Attributes	What it Means
<TABLE>	None	Signifies this is a table
<TR>	None	End of Table Row
<CAPTION>	None	Table Caption
<TH>	COLSPAN	Width in columns
	ROWSPAN	Height in rows
	ALIGN	Justification (left, right, center)
<TD>	COLSPAN	Width in columns
	ROWSPAN	Height in rows
	ALIGN	Justification (left, right, center)
<THEAD>,<TFOOT>,<TBODY>	CELLHALIGN	Horizontal Alignment
	CELLVALIGN	Vertical Alignment
<COLGROUP>	WIDTH	Column Grouping Width
	SPAN	Column Grouping Span

FIGURE 10.2 A complex, boxed table.

TABLE WIDTH AND ALIGNMENT

HTML gives you a good deal of control over the width and alignment of tables. Many of the table-alignment features now in HTML 4.0 were introduced by Netscape in its Version-3 browser.

TABLE WIDTH

The **WIDTH** attribute, together with the optional **UNITS** attribute, controls table width. You can express table width by using the **UNITS** attribute with either **PIXEL** (screen pixels) or **RELATIVE** (a percentage of the page width). To create a table that occupies half the width of the page, use HTML markup like this:

<TABLE WIDTH="50" UNITS="RELATIVE">

> **How Big Is a Pixel?** Remember, different screen resolutions will cause a table set to a fixed pixel width to look different.

Earlier, you learned about the COLSPAN and ROWSPAN attributes, which allow you to set the size of cells in your tables. In addition, the **<COL>** and **<COLGROUP>** elements allow you to apply width, alignment, and other attributes to *groups* of columns.

ALIGNMENT IN TABLES

Basic table alignment is controlled using the **ALIGN** attribute. For example, to center a table on your viewer's page, begin your table markup like this:

<TABLE ALIGN="CENTER">

HTML 4.0 introduces a great deal of additional control over the alignment of the information in the table cells themselves. Besides justification (which you've seen in Figure 10.2), you now have the ability to align text around a specific character, such as a decimal point in a cell, using the **CHAR** attribute. Also, you can use the **VALIGN** attribute to control vertical alignment in cells. Finally, the **<COLS>** and **<COLGROUP>** elements give you style-sheet-like control over alignment in groups of cells.

OTHER NEW TABLE FEATURES IN HTML 4.0

The HTML 4.0 standard also adds a number of other new features to its table support. These include:

- International Language Support, including text-flow direction (see Lesson 23, "Other Aspects of HTML 4.0")

- Labeling of cells, with the **AXIS** and **AXES** attributes, for use by speech synthesizers in interpreting tables for the visually impaired

- Table Headers (**THEAD**) and Footers (**TFOOT**), which remain in place as a table is scrolled

- Flexible table border (that is, the frame that surrounds a table) and internal ruling features with **FRAME** and **RULE** attributes

- Control over the spacing between and within cells with the **CELLSPACING** and **CELLPADDING** attributes

ADVANCED, CREATIVE USE OF HTML TABLES

You probably don't need a table of data in every HTML document, and may be wondering why you should bother with all this table markup, one of the most complex subjects in HTML. In fact, many sophisticated HTML authors use table markup to overcome limitations in HTML for document layout.

> **TIP** **Not Just Numbers** Table cells can contain almost anything an HTML document can contain, including images, hyperlinks, and most other HTML markup.

In fact, HTML table markup creates many of the striking Web pages you've probably seen. Figure 10.3 shows a simple example, the Microsoft home page (**http://www.microsoft.com/**). If you take a look at the HTML source for this page, you'll see it's mostly done in tables. For example, the black toolbar across the top of the window consists of a table containing eight images, seven of which are clickable hyperlinks. You'll want to use your Web browser's **View Source** capability to study this code, but let's get an idea of what they've done here.

Take a detailed look at the HTML source for this table. You'll see several important capabilities:

- Graphical images can be placed inside table cells, with full control of height, width, and alignment.

- Images and other data inside a table cell can also be clickable hyperlinks, using the anchor tag.

- Alignment of the table is fine-tuned with the CELLPADDING attribute.

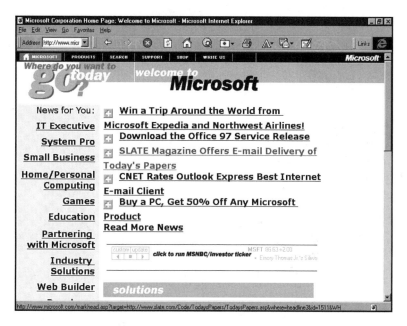

FIGURE 10.3   Microsoft home page, featuring table markup.

In this lesson, we focused on HTML tables, with basic table setup information, as well as examples of sophisticated table markup by using images and other HTML capabilities within tables to create striking effects. In the next lesson, we'll turn to adding images to your Web pages.

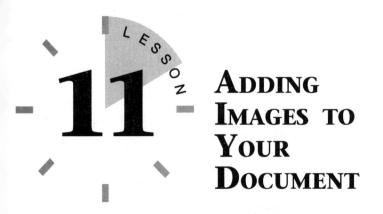

ADDING IMAGES TO YOUR DOCUMENT

In this lesson, you learn to include colorful images, such as your company logo, in your HTML documents, and to make them hyperlinks.

ADDING AN IN-LINE IMAGE

There are two sorts of images used in HTML documents. Those that appear directly in your document are called **in-line images**. Other images, called **external images**, will be discussed later.

Most Web browsers can handle just a few kinds of in-line images:

- **Graphic Interchange Format (GIF)** images

- **Joint Photographic Experts Group (JPEG)** image type (now supported by most browsers)

- **X Windows** images, (normally found on UNIX systems) called **X-Bitmap (XBM) images**, a black-and-white image type

- Color **X-Pixelmap (XPM)** images, another X Windows image type

Other image types not directly supported by a browser are treated as external images, viewable with a **helper application** or **plug-in**, add-on software you'll learn about in Lesson 13, "Helper Applications and Plug-Ins for Multimedia."

As with other HTML markup, you include an in-line image using markup tags. The minimal image inclusion tag is this:

<IMG SRC=*"filename"*>

> **Whoa, There! What About <OBJECT>?** HTML 4.0's new tag for including images is **<OBJECT>**. <OBJECT> is a more comprehensive tag that applies not only to images, but also, more generally, to the **inclusion** of some kind of data object in a Web page. <IMG> still works, but bear in mind that <OBJECT> can be substituted wherever it appears. At the time this book was being written, neither Internet Explorer 4's Preview Release nor Netscape Version 4.03 supported the use of <OBJECT> for image inclusion, and we'll use < IMG> throughout this lesson.

As you can see, image inclusion requires the attribute **SRC**, since it specifies your image. Also, the file name of your image appears to the right of the equal sign.

Providing ALT Text

Users with slower connections to the Internet, such as dial-up modem connections, often turn off auto-loading of images. Others use **text-only** Web browsers like **Lynx**, with no graphical capabilities. The **ALT** attribute allows you to specify a text string to appear in place of the image for these users, in order to make your pages usable in these circumstances. For example, if you've included your company's logo, provide alternative text for users with nongraphical browsers like this:

<IMG ALT="[Company Logo]"
SRC="mycompany.gif">

Web pages consisting of nothing but images are completely useless to a nongraphical browser, so it's a good idea to include the ALT attribute in all <IMG> tags.

ALIGNING YOUR IN-LINE IMAGES

HTML 4.0 style sheets allow you to control the alignment of your in-line images. With style sheets, images (and other objects) are said to **float** on the HTML page, and you can place them with the **ALIGN** attribute. Here's an example:

> **<IMG ALT="[Logo]" ALIGN="center"**
> **SRC="company.gif">**

Other ALIGN values are **left** (the default) and **right**. HTML 4.0 alignment allows for the text on your HTML pages to flow around in-line images, according to the following rules:

- Left alignment causes subsequent text in the document to flow down along the image's right side.

- Center alignment causes text to flow first along the left side of the image, then resume on the right side.

- Right alignment causes text to flow down the left side of the image.

Figure 11.1 shows all three kinds of image alignment.

> **Three on a Match** What you see in Figure 11.1 doesn't exactly match the preceding descriptions, especially with respect to center alignment. This shows, despite Microsoft's claims to the contrary, Internet Explorer 4 doesn't fully support the HTML 4.0 standard. (Netscape Version 4.03 also does not support image alignment as described here, but then again Netscape 4.03 doesn't purport to be HTML 4.0-compliant.)

In addition to this basic alignment/text-flow control, you can fine-tune your text flow around images with HTML 4.0. You can specify what happens with the text flowing around your images when a line break occurs, using HTML style-sheet markup. Your choice comes down to whether you want a line break to continue the flow or return to the margin. Here's an example of embedded-style-sheet markup (recall, embedded style sheets must appear somewhere in the <HEAD> section of an HTML document):

<STYLE TYPE="text/css">

BR { clear: left }

</STYLE>

With this markup, line breaks (
, <P>, or any other line breaking tag) will return the text to the left margin; using "none" rather than "left" in the example will allow your text to continue flowing down/around your image, even after line breaks. As of this writing, Internet Explorer did not support this aspect of HTML 4.0.

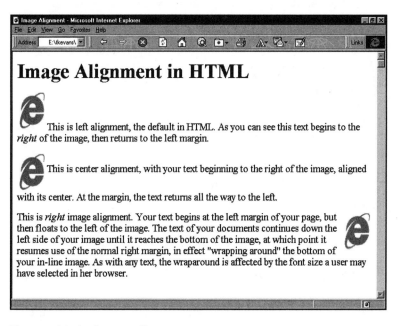

FIGURE 11.1   Image alignment.

USING **HEIGHT** AND **WIDTH**

Ordinarily, Web browsers have to download images before they can identify their on-screen size. This results in delays in the display of your HTML documents, as the user's browser waits to learn the size of images before displaying the text of the document. You can reserve space for your in-line images using the **HEIGHT** and **WIDTH** attributes, causing your HTML documents to load faster, as Web browsers leave enough space for the images, and go ahead with the text while the images are downloading.

Both HEIGHT and WIDTH are specified using screen pixels, and should be the same size as the actual image. For example, the Internet Explorer logo in Figure 11.1 is 64×80 pixels. Here's an HTML fragment using HEIGHT and WIDTH:

> **<IMG ALIGN="LEFT" HEIGHT="80" WIDTH="64" SRC="ie.gif">**

MAKING AN IN-LINE IMAGE A HYPERLINK

In Lesson 8, "Using Anchors and Links," you learned to use the HTML anchor **<A>** tag to create highlighted hyperlinks leading to other documents or to URLs representing services elsewhere on the World Wide Web. HTML authors frequently use in-line images themselves as hyperlinks by inserting the <IMG> tag within the anchor. Here is an example:

> **<A HREF="http://sales.mycompany.com/"><IMG ALT="[Sales Department Logo]" ALIGN="LEFT" HEIGHT="32" WIDTH="32" SRC="sales.gif">Sales Department</A>**

In this example, we've included a hyperlink to an URL pointing to Sales' Web server. The image itself and the text "Sales Department" are the highlighted hyperlink displayed on the Web page.

> **TIP**
>
> **Slide into Home**   Insert the complete <IMG> tag, with several attributes, between the URL and the highlighted text to use the image as a hyperlink. Use of the ALT attribute ensures nongraphical browser users will be able to use the page.

When you view this in a browser, you'll see not only the normal clickable text highlighted, but also the image itself is highlighted. Click directly on the image to access the hyperlink.

THUMBNAIL IMAGES LINK TO EXTERNAL IMAGES

Besides the obvious uses of images as hyperlinks, you can also link a small in-line image, sometimes called a **thumbnail image**, with a larger, **external** version of the same image. This saves on the network bandwidth required to load the HTML document. If the reader wants to, he can click the hyperlinked thumbnail to see the larger image. Here is an example anchor:

```
<A HREF="bigimage.gif"><IMG ALT="[Logo]"
SRC="thumbnail.gif">View Large Image (150kb)
</A>
```

As you can see, we've linked directly to the external image, along with adding a reference to the image size to tip off the user to the fact that clicking the thumbnail downloads a large file.

WHAT HAPPENS WHEN A USER CAN'T VIEW IMAGES?

We've already covered use of ALT for including text to display in place of in-line images in nongraphical Web browsers. Not only is it always a good idea to include the ALT attribute, you should always include text hyperlinks as alternatives to image links for the same reasons. Presenting a Web page with nothing but a lot of

[IMAGE] links is most unfriendly to those with plain-text browsers. And, as we'll see in the next section, there are other reasons for providing text-based alternatives to images, even to users with graphical browsers.

OTHER IMAGE-RELATED CONSIDERATIONS

Now that you know how easy it is to include images in your Web pages, it's tempting to start throwing images at your users. Before you do, take a few minutes to consider some of the ramifications of images.

IMAGE SIZE

Many people who access the Web do so over high-speed network links, but others use dial-up modems and telephone lines. Even with incredible advances in modem technology, today's fastest modems are still very slow compared with local area networks (LANs) and leased digital lines.

Images can be very large, and take time to download. It will take longer to retrieve and render your document if it contains many large images. This may only be a few seconds on your LAN, but may be much longer over a modem link. Experts disagree on the appropriate image size, or the overall size of a page with multiple images, but follow these guidelines:

- Slow-loading Web pages often result in impatient users going elsewhere. If you rely on your Web server as a sales or service tool, this is obviously not a welcome development.

- Make sure your HTML documents are fully functional in a text-only environment, so when your images aren't available, your hyperlinks still work. The hyperlink to the company sales department in the previous example contains *both an image and highlighted text,* either of which can be selected to follow the hyperlink.

Even if all your customers have high-speed network links, there are issues of quality involved, too. Inclusion of a large number of images can create an overall look you may not like. Imagine the worst commercial strip in your town or city, with neon and other signs scattered helter-skelter advertising car dealerships, motels, adult bookstores, and fast-food restaurants—and make sure your Web pages don't look like it.

> **It's All in the Content**   Beginning HTML authors who're learning all the great features of the language frequently lose sight of the main point of Web pages. No amount of fancy images and other HTML tricks will cover up for a Web page that has little or no substantive content. If you make users wait while large images (or Java applets/ActiveX controls) download, and give them no real information in the end, they'll surely go elsewhere.

CREATING IMAGES

Finally, people wonder how to create images, and where they can obtain images others have created. Images can be created using 3-D, paint, and image manipulation software, such as Paint Shop Pro, ImageMagick, Photoshop, and others. Macintosh users know screen snapshots are easy with no special software.

You can also:

- Use a scanner and scanner software to scan photos or other images

- Take images from clip art collections

- Download and save images you find on the Web

- Use one of the new digital cameras to make your vacation or other photos into images

Remember, your images must be in one of the standard formats (listed in the "Adding an In-Line Image" section earlier in this lesson) in order for them to be usable as in-line images. The software packages mentioned previously (as well as others) have the capability of converting images among a wide variety of formats, so incompatible images you may have can easily be turned into usable ones.

Remember the Copyright   If you take images from a clip art collection or use a scanner, be sure to observe copyrights.

This lesson covered the basics of images in HTML. You learned how to add and align in-line images; how to include alternative text for users without Web browsers or those with low-bandwidth links; and how to hyperlink in-line images to other documents or external images. In the next lesson, we'll extend our work with images.

CREATING CLICKABLE IMAGE MAPS

*In this lesson, you learn one of the
most exciting features of HTML: clickable image maps containing
hyperlinks in the images. Image maps contain "hot spots," each of
which is a hyperlink to a different document or location.*

INTRODUCTION

You've undoubtedly seen **clickable**, or **hot**, **images** on the
Web; in fact, they're so common anymore as to be almost unre-
markable. These are images with hyperlinks built right into them,
so that when you click the image, you jump to another HTML
document. Even more exciting, depending on where in the image
you click, you go to a different URL. An example might be a
floorplan of an office building, in which clicking a suite in the
map might generate a detailed floorplan of that suite.

There are two ways of using image maps:

- Traditional *server-side* image maps, controlled by the Web
  server from which they come.

- *Client-side* image maps, activated by Web browsers from
  HTML markup.

Client-side image maps offer substantial advantages, but are not
supported in the older Web browsers. As a result, you'll want to
be familiar with each.

LAYOUT OF IMAGE MAPS

Both methods are based on the same preliminary measurement and layout of your image hot spots, using methods you'll recall from high school algebra. Image map hot spots are laid out using screen pixel coordinates on a horizontal-vertical axis. That is, if there is a rectangular area in the image you want to be a clickable area, you'll need to get the x-y coordinates of two corners of the rectangle and record them. While this is a potentially tedious process, there are several shareware and commercial programs available which make it easy:

- *Mapedit* (for PCs and UNIX systems, available at **http://www.boutell.com/mapedit/**)

- *WebMap* (for Macs, at **http://home.city.net/cnx/software/webmap.html**)

- LiveImage (for Windows 95/NT, available at **http://www.mediatec.com/**)

These packages use graphical interfaces in which you use your mouse to outline the hot spots in your image, capturing the coordinates. They automate much of the process of setting up image maps. Figure 12.1 shows a **Mapedit** session; note the toolbar at the top of the image, with buttons for drawing rectangles, polygons, and circles. Clicking one of these buttons allows you to use your mouse to define your hotspot, just by dragging it over the region in your image.

> **Keep It Small**   As with other images in your Web pages, keep your image maps small so people don't get impatient with lengthy downloads. You'll also want to provide a plain-text alternative to your image maps to ensure everyone can use them.
>
> *TIP*

FIGURE 12.1 Mapedit.

Once you have your coordinates, create an image map file containing them and URLs to correspond to them. Here's an example:

> **rect http://www.company.com/bk1.html**
> **150,337 177,346**
>
> **rect http://www.company.com/bk2.html**
> **184,286 220,314**
>
> **rect http://www.company.com/bk3.html**
> **330,102 350,150**
>
> **default http:/www.company.com/bookhelp.html**

As you can see, each entry contains a keyword for the shape of the hot spot (in this example, **rect**). Next, you see familiar URLs. Finally, the file contains the x-y coordinates for the upper-left and lower-right of the rectangles. (Polygons require four or more coordinates, while circles require just a center coordinate and a radius.) You'll want to add a **default** URL, as shown, to be accessed when the user clicks outside of your hot spot(s).

> **TIP**   **On Automatic**   Mapedit, LiveImage, and WebMac create the image map file for you based on your selected hot spots. Pop-up dialog boxes prompt you for the URL to associate with your hot spots.

Setting Up Server-Side Image Maps on Your Web Server

If you're using server-side image maps, now's the time to get your local WebMaster involved. Each clickable image map available on your Web server needs to be registered with the server before it will be active. To do this on the Apache server, add it to the server's configuration files. (Check your server documentation for details, or for instructions for setting up image maps on other Web server software.) Here's a sample entry for Apache:

bookshelf   : /web-docs/bookshelf.map

This file is very simple. On the left of the colon is a **nickname** by which you want the map known to the server; you'll use the nickname in your HTML markup. On the right is the directory path on your server to the map file you created earlier by hand or with Mapedit or WebMap.

HTML Markup for Image Maps

The simplest step in setting up your image maps is your HTML document markup. Markup for server-side and client-side image maps differ, though you can use both. We'll cover both methods.

HTML MARKUP FOR SERVER-SIDE IMAGE MAPS

Let's look at HTML containing markup for a server-side image map first, and then build our way to client-side markup. The following HTML fragment sets up an image map we've nicknamed *bookshelf.*

> **<A HREF="http://www.yourcompany.com/cgi-bin/ imagemap/bookshelf"><IMG ALT="[Bookshelf Image]" SRC="bookshelf.gif" ISMAP></A>**

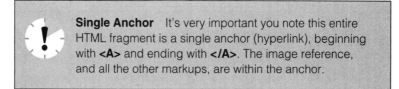

Single Anchor It's very important you note this entire HTML fragment is a single anchor (hyperlink), beginning with **<A>** and ending with **</A>**. The image reference, and all the other markups, are within the anchor.

The URL in this fragment is a little strange. Besides the familiar URL service name, we've tacked on **cgi-bin/imagemap/bookshelf**. Your Web server runs a program called *imagemap*. (You'll learn more about the Common Gateway Interface in Lesson 14, "Fill-In Forms and CGI Scripts.") Here, we've called the *imagemap* program with our *bookshelf* nickname.

Second, we've added the new **ISMAP** attribute to indicate the image is a clickable image map. When users click an image map, the coordinates of the click location are sent to the Web server and the imagemap program runs, sending back the URL associated with the hot spot.

HTML MARKUP FOR CLIENT-SIDE IMAGE MAPS

While server-side image maps work with your image hot spot coordinates stored in files on the Web server, client-side maps include them right in the HTML document. Let's look at an example, and then take it apart.

> **<MAP NAME="bookshelf"><AREA SHAPE="RECT" COORDS="150,337,177,346" HREF="http:// www.yourcompany.com/bk1.html">**

```
<AREA SHAPE="RECT" COORDS="184,286,220,314"
HREF="http://www.company.com/bk2.html">
</MAP>
```

This is quite an HTML mouthful, so let's break it down. First, note the new **<MAP>** tag and its attribute **NAME**, where we've used the now-familiar *bookshelf* nickname. The **<AREA>** tag (two of them are shown) is also a new one, as are its two attributes, **SHAPE** and **COORDS**. AREA signifies an image map hot spot, while SHAPE and COORDS define it by using x-y coordinates.

Slight Difference   Note the syntax of the x-y coordinates is slightly different from that of the image map file shown previously, with commas separating the pairs of coordinates, rather than spaces.

You need one more bit of HTML magic to associate your marked-off image map with the image itself.

```
<IMG ALT="[Bookshelf Image]"
SRC="bookshelf.gif" USEMAP=#bookshelf>
```

Most of this is familiar to you, as it signifies an in-line image. What's new here is **USEMAP**. Much like ISMAP, which you used earlier in your server-side image map markup, USEMAP tells your Web browser a client-side image map nicknamed *bookshelf* is to be used. The browser will locate the <MAP> markup and the *bookshelf* nickname within the HTML page itself, *without contacting the Web server*. When the user clicks an image hot spot, the browser retrieves the URL associated with the hot spot coordinates.

USING BOTH SERVER- AND CLIENT-SIDE IMAGE MAPS

If part of your Web server's clientele is using Web browsers which don't support client-side image maps, you may want to use both methods so everyone can take advantage of your image. Here's an example:

> **<A HREF="http://www.yourcompany.com/cgi-bin/ imagemap/bookshelf"><IMG ALT="[Bookshelf Image]" SRC="bookshelf.gif" ISMAP USEMAP="#bookshelf"></A>**

Here, both kinds of image map markup are included. Older Web browsers, which don't understand client-side image maps, will just ignore the unknown markup (including the <MAP> tag) and zero in on what they do recognize, namely, <ISMAP> and the server-side image map markup. Newer browsers choose client-side method when both are presented.

> **Keep In Sync**   You'll need to make sure your WebMaster keeps the server-side image map files on the Web server in sync with the client-side image map markup in your HTML code. If your coordinates or images change, for ex-ample, the changes need to be reflected in both locations.

WHICH TO USE, SERVER- OR CLIENT-SIDE IMAGE MAPS?

As you might have guessed from the previous section, the Web browser being used by your Web server's clientele may dictate the need for you to have both server- and client-side image maps (or only server-side maps).

Client-side image maps have substantial advantages, and you should use them to the extent you can. For one thing, you have full control over your image maps, and don't have to coordinate with your WebMaster everytime you change or add image maps.

Moreover, there are important technical advantages to client-side image maps. Web browsers don't need to send the coordinates of the mouse click off to the Web server for interpretation. Rather, since the URLs associated with the hot spot coordinates are right in the HTML markup, *all the coordinate processing is done by the browser*, which directly retrieves the URL. In server-side image maps, the browser sends off the coordinates to the server, which looks them up in the server image map file, then sends back the URL associated with them. A busy or remote server, or a busy network, can delay response with server-side image maps.

Creating clickable image maps has been the subject of this lesson. You've learned the necessary HTML markup to specify an image map, the process of laying out the "hot spots" in your image and linking them to URLs (including important tools for automating your image), and the changes necessary on your Web server to make your clickable maps active. In the next lesson, we'll discuss Web browser helper applications and plug-ins for the inclusion of multimedia—video and sound—in your HTML documents.

HELPER APPLICATIONS AND PLUG-INS FOR MULTIMEDIA

In this lesson, you learn how Helper applications and plug-ins allow you to incorporate multimedia (audio and video) into your HTML documents.

HELPER APPLICATIONS AND PLUG-INS

We mentioned Helper applications and plug-ins briefly in Lesson 3, "Understanding Web Browsers." These are separate programs browsers use to deal with data they retrieve from a Web server that isn't directly supported. Most Web browsers support HTML documents, plain text, and several kinds of in-line images, but they require other programs for multimedia, like sound, video, and other kinds of data.

 Helper Applications These take the data Web browsers can't interpret and deal with it, whether displaying unsupported images or playing sound or video files, by calling up a new window to display the data. Microsoft refers to Helper applications as **Viewers**.

Plug-Ins   Plug-ins perform much the same role as Helper applications, but are more tightly integrated into Web browsers. Rather than popping up a new window for the multimedia data, they are displayed right in the browser window.

INSTALLING AND SETTING UP HELPER APPLICATIONS

While Web browsers can call up Helper applications for multimedia, the Helpers must first be installed on the computer. And, once a Helper application is installed, the Web browser must be told to use it. Here's the procedure.

Most browsers have a **Preferences** (Netscape) or **Options** (Internet Explorer) dialog box for setting up links between the Helper applications and the types of multimedia. Older browsers may require editing of a simple text file on your system. Figure 13.1 shows Internet Explorer's Options dialog box for Helper applications; to open it, pull down the **View** menu and select **Options**, click the **Programs** tab and, finally, click **File Types** in the right center of the Programs popup. Here, you can see and edit the Viewers/Helpers you already have installed, and add new ones. Here, the Adobe Acrobat reader is shown as the selected Helper application.

You can find dozens of Helper applications at: **http:// www.yahoo.com/Computers_and_Internet/Software/ Internet/World_Wide_Web/Browsers/ Helper_Applications/**. Other places to look include:

- **http://www.browsers.com/**
- **http://www.tucows.com/**

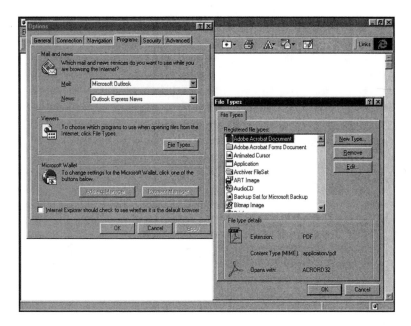

FIGURE 13.1   Microsoft Viewers dialog box.

INSTALLING AND CONFIGURING PLUG-INS

Plug-ins, a new Web browser feature supported in Netscape and Internet Explorer, offer what is, in many ways, an improved way of accessing data, such as multimedia, not directly supported by Web browsers. (Microsoft disparages plug-ins as passé, though, pushing instead for its new **ActiveX** controls, about which you'll learn in Lesson 17, "Active Web Pages with Java and ActiveX.") Plug-in software manufacturers do all the hard work in building the applications. Installing and configuring them, especially on PCs, is as simple as running the Setup program that comes with the software. Once you've done that, your Web browser automatically knows about and can use your new plug-in.

While early plug-ins, such as Macromedia's ShockWave, were almost exclusively multimedia players, this fast-moving market segment is generating a growing list of other kinds of plug-ins.

Check out the growing lists of plug-ins on the Web at **http://home.netscape.com/comprods/products/navigator/version_2.0/plugins/** (directly accessible from Netscape's pull-down **Help** menu) or Yahoo!'s listing at **http://www.yahoo.com/Computers_and_Internet/Software/Internet/World_Wide_Web/Browsers/**. In either place, you'll find hundreds of available plug-ins.

Netscape has made Plug-in Software Development Kits for Windows, OS/2, the Macintosh, and UNIX systems available for free download. You can use these to develop your own plug-ins.

HTML MARKUP FOR MULTIMEDIA

Now that you know what Helper applications and plug-ins are, let's turn to the HTML markup you need to make them work.

You already know most of what you need to include multimedia in your HTML. You know how to use hyperlinks in your documents to point to other documents or to Internet services. Creating a hyperlink to an audio, video, or other multimedia file works exactly the same way. Here's a made-up example that includes both audio and video:

> **<HTML><HEAD><TITLE>Audio and Video </TITLE></HEAD>**
>
> **<BODY><H1>Audio and Video</H1>**
>
> **You can view a movie clip of <A HREF="http://www.hawaii-50.com/hawaii.mpg">beautiful Hawaii</A> or <A HREF="http://www.hawaii-50.com/ocean.au">listen to the roar of the surf </A>.**

As you can see, this example uses hyperlinks to point to multimedia files; the links are the same as any other hyperlink. There are no special HTML markup tags or other HTML-specific requirements to link in these, or any other kind of multimedia files. Just create the links and you're done. Users with suitably equipped computers (you need a sound card and speakers to listen to audio clips, for instance) will be able to view and hear your multimedia links, via either a Helper application or a plug-in.

> **Size Concerns** Even very short audio and video clips can be extremely large, in the range of megabytes (millions of bytes) in length. This is much larger than most of the images you will be adding to your HTML documents. Compression technology is working toward making these large files easier to download, even over slow network links, but you need to be aware of the size of your multimedia files.

BROWSERS, HELPERS, PLUG-INS, AND MIME

Web servers are set up to know about a list of common **file types**, including most widely used types of multimedia files, using a mechanism called **MIME**, or **Multipurpose Internet Mail Extensions**. When a Web server sends data to a browser, it first consults its list of MIME file types and then tells the requesting client what type of data is coming.

> **MIME** You may have run across MIME in the context of e-mail, where it's used to allow attachment of non-text files to e-mail messages for transmission over the Internet, which normally requires all e-mail to be in plain text. Eudora is one MIME-compliant, e-mail package.

The Web browser reads the incoming file type information and tries to process it. If the data type isn't directly supported by the browser, the browser consults its list of Helper applications/plug-ins for the incoming data type. For example, if a Macintosh Web browser is configured to use a QuickTime video viewer to render incoming QuickTime video, the browser recognizes the incoming data and calls up the QuickTime viewer to play it.

Download Disappointment   Users sometimes wait for several minutes while a video or audio file downloads, and then nothing happens, or an error message occurs. This is usually an indication that the multimedia format isn't supported on your computer, the Web browser wasn't set up to use the correct Helper application/plug-in, or the Helper application/plug-in was not installed. Some recent browsers will ask you what to do with the data, while in some cases, you'll be prompted to download the necessary plug-in on the spot.

Fortunately, most Web browsers come with a preset list of MIME file types, and the file types are associated with the correct Helper applications/plug-ins. Users can always add to this list, but the critical step is getting and installing the necessary Helper applications and plug-ins.

Which Is Better—Helper Applications or Plug-Ins?

You might be wondering why you need to know about both Helper applications and plug-ins, and whether you can't just go with the latest rage, plug-ins. For multimedia purposes, plug-ins do offer the best mechanism, but only if everyone accessing your HTML documents is using a Web browser that supports plug-ins. Users with older browsers still need to use the traditional Helper application mechanism to view multimedia.

Helper applications have a strong advantage over plug-ins in a different area, however. The Helper application mechanism is much more flexible and adaptable to a wide variety of computer software applications. Virtually any software package can be set up quite easily as a Web browser Helper application.

Building a plug-in is a heavy-duty programming job, while setting up, say, WordPerfect as a Helper application is a simple, point-and-click process. Helper applications can be especially valuable on a corporate intranet, because you can create sharable document libraries, a spreadsheet gallery, or other organizational resources, all accessible by using Web browser and Helper applications. For more information about Helper applications and intranets, see *Building an Intranet*, also by Tim Evans (ISBN 1-57521-071-1), published by Sams.net.

"Intranet" Is Not Misspelled   The term intranet is used to refer to the use of World Wide Web and related networking technologies *inside* a company to create internal corporate Webs for the purpose of the corporation's own work. You need not be connected to the Internet to have an intranet, though you may do both.

MULTIMEDIA FEATURES IN INTERNET EXPLORER

Although Internet Explorer supports both Helper applications and plug-ins, it also supports another means of viewing multimedia. HTML markup tags, supported by Explorer alone, allow you to add **soundtracks** or **in-line movies** to a Web page. Using the <BGSOUND> tag, you can add an audio file that's played whenever the HTML document containing it is accessed. The **DYNSRC** attribute to the <IMG> tag refers to an in-line movie. Neither <BGSOUND> nor DYNSRC requires a Helper application or plug-in; Explorer itself renders the soundtrack or in-line movie in the main Explorer window.

Your HTML markup for soundtracks and in-line movies is just
what you'd expect when using these new tags. Here's a fragment
from our Hawaii example from earlier in this lesson, modified to
include both:

<BGSOUND="http://www.hawaii-50.com/
ocean.wav">

<IMG DYNSRC="http://www/hawaii-50.com/
hawaii.avi">

Explorer will display the video inline, as well as play the audio
soundtrack.

> **Not in HTML 4.0**   <BGSOUND> and DYNSRC are not
> included in the HTML 4.0 standard. Microsoft continues to
> work on new multimedia features in Internet Explorer. Your
> copy of Explorer may support new capabilities by the time
> you read this.

In this lesson, we discussed Web browser Helper applications and
plug-ins. Our objective was the inclusion of multimedia, such as
video and audio, in your HTML documents. While inclusion of
multimedia in HTML documents is very simple, there are a number of considerations to keep in mind, including user hardware
and Web browser configuration, available Helper applications and
plug-ins, and the size of your files. In the next lesson, we'll get
into HTML fill-in forms for gathering user input and the scripts
they call up to process the input.

FILL-IN FORMS AND CGI SCRIPTS

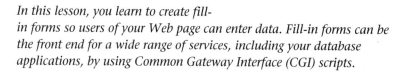

In this lesson, you learn to create fill-in forms so users of your Web page can enter data. Fill-in forms can be the front end for a wide range of services, including your database applications, by using Common Gateway Interface (CGI) scripts.

GETTING USER INPUT WITH FORMS

Besides including hyperlinks and images in your HTML documents, collecting user input by using fill-in forms is probably the most important feature of HTML. You can get input from users and feed it to computer programs for almost any purpose, like taking orders or updating a database.

CREATING HTML FILL-IN FORMS

HTML forms must be declared with the **<FORM>** markup tag.

I Declare   You'll recall from Lesson 4 the use of the <HTML> tag as a declaration of the document's overall HTML content; here we use <FORM> to announce the HTML document contains a form.

<FORM ACTION="URL" METHOD="post">

...Rest of Form...

</FORM>

We've shown the <FORM> tag with its *mandatory attribute*, **ACTION**, and the **METHOD** attribute. We'll discuss the ACTION attribute later, but bear in mind *an HTML form collects information from the user.* The ACTION attribute specifies what the Web server is to do with the information. In virtually all cases, the value of METHOD is **post**, so you can pretty much consider this a boilerplate.

Within an HTML page, include markup tags to create your form. This is done with a new HTML tag and two new attributes:

- **<INPUT>** tag. Collects and saves the data for the user so it can be passed off later.

- **NAME** attribute. Attaches an identifying label to the information.

- **TYPE** attribute. Signifies the type of action to be taken with the data.

In addition, since you're going to pass the collected information to another computer program, you must have a way the user can indicate completion of the form. Here is markup, added to the preceding <FORM> fragment to add these features:

<FORM ACTION="URL" METHOD="post"><INPUT NAME="somename">

...Rest of Form...

<INPUT TYPE="submit"></FORM>

In this fragment, we've added NAME and TYPE attributes to the two <INPUT> tags and added a temporary label for the data to be input, *somename.*

There are several ways to collect information from a user. These include:

- Fill-in-the-blanks

- Check boxes

- Radio buttons

- Pull-down or scrollable menus

Radio buttons   The push buttons on most car radios can be set to select different stations. Pressing one of them not only selects the station you want, but also *deselects* all others. You can only press one radio button at a time. Radio buttons in HTML forms work the same way.

Applying Fill-In-the-Blank

Having a user fill in a blank is the simplest way to get information. The **TEXT** attribute accomplishes this:

> **<FORM ACTION="URL" METHOD="post">Please Enter Your Name:<INPUT TYPE="text" SIZE=20 NAME="yourname">**
>
> **<INPUT TYPE="submit"></FORM>**

Here, we've created a simple one-line box, 20 characters wide, and asked the user to type into it. In addition, we've provided a button for the user to click to submit the information. Let's take a look at this basic form in Figure 14.1.

Using Check Boxes and Radio Buttons

Besides a simple text box, it's useful to present the user with a set of **predefined choices**. HTML forms markup allows a couple of ways to do this.

The **CHECKBOX** attribute allows the user to select *one or more* of several choices, while the **RADIO** attribute allows the choice of *just one* of several. Like the TEXT attribute, both of these require the attribute NAME, and both allow you to preselect **default** selections for the user. Here's a piece of HTML containing both:

> **<FORM ACTION="URL" METHOD="post">Choose Your Favorite Ice Cream Flavor(s):<INPUT TYPE="CHECKBOX" NAME="flavors" VALUE="chocolate" CHECKED>Chocolate<INPUT TYPE="CHECKBOX" NAME="flavors"**

VALUE="vanilla">Vanilla<INPUT
TYPE="CHECKBOX" NAME="flavors"
VALUE="strawberry">Strawberry

<P>Choose a topping (only one, please):

<P><INPUT TYPE="RADIO" NAME="topping"
VALUE="hotfudge">Hot Fudge
<INPUT
TYPE="RADIO" NAME="topping"
VALUE="marshmallow"
CHECKED>Marshmallow
<INPUT
TYPE="RADIO" NAME="topping"
VALUE="butterscotch">Butterscotch
<INPUT
TYPE="RADIO" NAME="topping"
VALUE="pineapple">Pineapple

<P><INPUT TYPE="submit" VALUE="Order
Sundae"><INPUT TYPE="reset"></FORM>

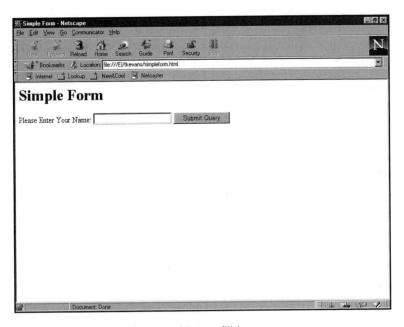

Figure 14.1 Simple form with text fill-in.

This is a fairly long listing, with several new items in it, so let's take a look at Figure 14.2, which is a screenshot of the resulting form.

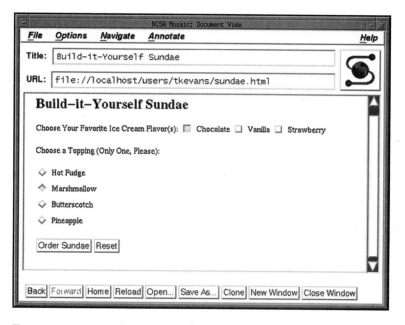

FIGURE 14.2   The user can choose as many check boxes as he wants, but only one radio button.

We've added a new button to the bottom of this form, next to the *Order Sundae* button, labeled *Reset*. **Reset** returns the form to its default selections, just in case you can't decide and want to start over. In addition, we've replaced the generic "submit query" text with our custom "Order Sundae" button, using a **VALUE** attribute. You'll also note we've laid out the choices in two different ways, one horizontal and the other vertical, using the <P> (paragraph) and
 (line break) tags, showing how other HTML markup lets you set up forms pretty much any way you'd like.

What's in a Name   Let's touch for a moment on the **NAME** attributes in the preceding form. When the user has completed and submitted the form, these values get passed to the CGI program for which the form is the front end.

PROVIDING PULL-DOWN MENUS AND SCROLLBOXES

If check boxes or radio buttons aren't satisfactory, there are other ways to lay out choices, using the **<SELECT>** tag and its companion **<OPTION>**. You can provide users with pull-down menus and scrollboxes with multiple choices. Let's rework our Build-it-Yourself Sundae form using these tags, so you can see the difference.

<H1>Build-it-Yourself Sundae</H1>
<FORM ACTION="URL" METHOD="post">

Choose Your Favorite Ice Cream Flavor(s). Press CTRL-Click for multiple flavors:

<SELECT NAME="flavors" MULTIPLE>
<OPTION SELECTED>Chocolate <OPTION>Vanilla

<OPTION>Strawberry

<OPTION>Cookies 'n Cream</SELECT>

<P>Choose a Topping (Only One, Please)

<SELECT NAME="topping">
<OPTION SELECTED>Marshmallow

<OPTION>Hot Fudge

<OPTION>Marshmallow

<OPTION>Butterscotch

<OPTION>Pineapple</SELECT>

Figure 14.3 shows the revised form. You'll note the first selection shows the four choices in a box, from which the user can select one or more items. (Had there been more choices, the selection box would've shown a scroll bar.) In the second selection, the button labeled "Marshmallow" covers a menu; clicking it (as has been done in Figure 14.3) raises a menu of the four choices. As before, defaults are already set.

FIGURE 14.3   Our form takes on a different look with selection boxes and pull-down menus.

COLLECTING EXTENDED USER INPUT

There's one final—and very useful—HTML element for collecting user input. You've already seen the TEXT attribute, which provides a single-line text box. Suppose, however, you want more than just a single line, and you can't predict just how much information the user might enter. **TEXTAREA** allows you to provide a freeform, multiline text box in which users can type to their hearts' content.

TEXTAREA requires a **NAME** attribute and allows for sizing both in width (**COLS**) and height (**ROWS**). Here's an HTML fragment illustrating this:

> **Please type your comments into the box below, pressing RETURN at the end of each line. When you are finished, press <EM>Submit Suggestion</EM>. Press <EM>Reset</EM> to clear the form and start over.**
>
> **<TEXTAREA NAME="comments" COLS=40 ROWS=8></TEXTAREA>**
>
> **<P><INPUT TYPE="submit" VALUE="Submit Suggestion"><INPUT TYPE="reset"></P>**

The TEXTAREA element is shown in Figure 14.4. Here, we've provided an 8-line, 40-row box for comments.

Pushing the Envelope   The TEXTAREA size, specified with COLS and ROWS, affects only what's displayed by the user's Web browser. As you might guess from the horizontal and vertical scroll bars, the user can continue typing in the form, even beyond the right margin, and can enter more than eight lines of text.

OTHER FORMS FEATURES

There are several other things you can do with HTML forms, including:

- Prompt the user for a user name and password before permitting the form data to be submitted.

- Include some hidden information (neither entered nor seen by the user) for session tracking. The hidden information, such as which Web browser the user is running, gets passed to the back-end script.

- Include nearly any HTML markup, including clickable images, in a form.

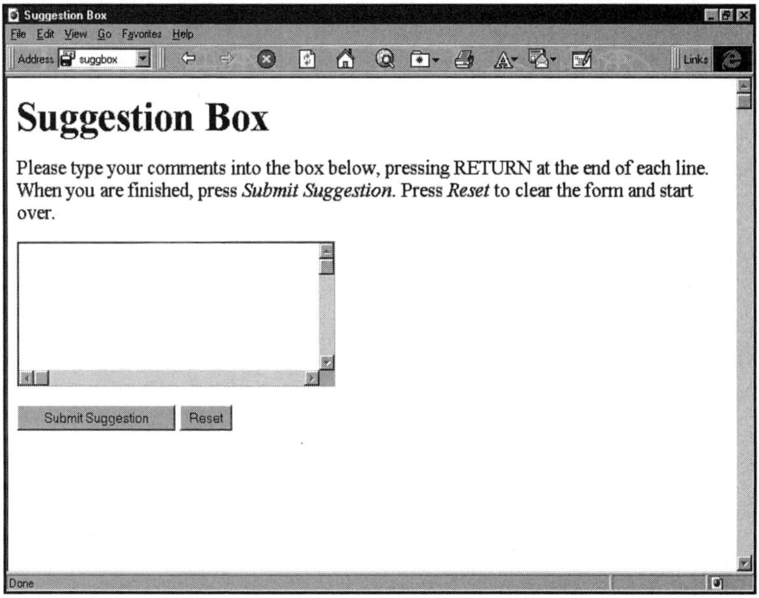

FIGURE 14.4   Users enter as much as they want with TEXTAREA.

NEW FORMS FEATURES IN HTML 4.0

Now that you're clued in to the basics of forms markup, you'll want to know about several new forms features in HTML 4.0.

<BUTTON>

The most visible new forms feature is the **<BUTTON>** tag. Prior to HTML 4.0, only two kinds of buttons were allowed, <SUBMIT> and <RESET>, and only two buttons (one of each) were allowed on any one form. <BUTTON> can be used to define as many buttons as you like. In addition, HTML 4.0 buttons can themselves include HTML markup—even images.

Finally, you can associate scripts (such as JavaScript code) with <BUTTON>. Doing so allows your forms to act on so-called *intrinsic events*, such as the mouse movements or clicks.

Keyboard Shortcuts in Forms

While most users are accustomed to using a mouse to move from one part of a form to another, it may be useful to set up a form so a single keystroke, such as the Tab key or an ALT+key combination, moves the **focus** of the form from one form field to another. The new **accesskey** attribute allows you to define such a key.

Data Checking

Prior to HTML 4.0, the only way to check for valid data in a form was to submit it to the Web server and let the CGI-bin script do this dirty work. Now, you can associate **client-side** scripts with intrinsic events to do validity checks right inside the form, so the user is notified immediately of bad data without the overhead of the round trip to the Web server.

Disabled/Read-Only Fields

It's often useful not only to have some fields in fill-in forms pre-set, but also to deny users the ability to change their contents. Prior to HTML 4.0, the only way to do this in forms was to use the hidden attribute. Now, you can set fields to be **read-only**. In addition, you can temporarily **disable** fields, and then re-enable them conditionally. One example of the latter is allowing one field to be filled in only if another one has been filled in first.

FIELD GROUPING

The new **<FIELDSET>** and **<LEGEND>** tags allow you to associate groups of form fields so they can be treated collectively. One use for this feature is in setting keyboard shortcuts for parts of a form, but not all of one. In addition, these tags will enable speech synthesizer software to improve the accessibility of forms for the visually impaired.

USING THE COMMON GATEWAY INTERFACE (CGI)

Now you know how to collect information with HTML forms, so we can spend a bit of time learning about processing it. As you learned earlier, the basic concept is taking the information entered on the form and passing it to the Web server. The **Common Gateway Interface (CGI)** is the standard way of doing so. While CGI is far too complex a subject to treat in this *10 Minute Guide*, you need to know some basics as you create HTML forms.

Our form examples have contained a so-far unexplained ACTION="URL" attribute. For forms, the URL is always the name of a program on the Web server. An example ACTION attribute might be:

> **ACTION="http://www.yourcompany.com/cgi-bin/ get_sundae"**

You can write CGI programs in almost any programming language, including:

- UNIX *shell*, *perl*, or *tcl* scripts
- DOS batch files
- Visual BASIC
- AppleScript
- C or C++ languages

Perl   Short for Larry Wall's **Practical Extraction and Report Language**, *perl* is the most widely used CGI-bin scripting language. It's freely available for most systems on which Web servers run, including PCs and Macs.

Tcl   The Tool Control Language, *tcl*, another interpreted scripting language, is also widely used for CGI programming. Like *perl*, *tcl* is available on a wide variety of computer systems, including PCs.

Whatever language you use, a CGI script must accept as input the information the user has entered into your form, and then process it in some way. The program may, to give a few examples:

- Send the information in an e-mail message to someone

- Query a database based on keywords entered in the form

- Enter the form data into a database (placing an online order, for example)

CGI scripts nearly always return their results in the form of HTML. To do this, your CGI script must format its output in HTML, including all necessary markup tags. The user's Web browser receives the HTML-formatted information and dynamically renders it for viewing. Most Web server software packages include example CGI scripts.

We've covered quite a bit of complex information in this lesson about HTML forms for gathering information from users. Also, we touched on the Common Gateway Interface for writing programs that take the information entered into forms and process it. The next lesson is about HTML Frames.

CREATING
FRAMES

*In this lesson, you'll learn about
Frames, a new HTML feature that will
liven up your documents.*

INTRODUCTION

HTML Frames, introduced with version 2 of Netscape Navigator
and subsequently embraced by Microsoft, has been extended in
HTML 4.0 to add new features and to provide alternative viewing
for browsers without Frames support.

WHAT ARE FRAMES?

Frames are much like the split-screen video tricks used by television networks to retain viewers between shows. You've seen these,
where part of the screen shows the ending show's credits, while
the other shows a teaser for the next show. HTML Frames allow
the Web browser window to be sectioned off into independent,
interactive Frames.

Frames can contain ordinary HTML markup, be scrollable, and
even be clickable images or image maps. While you interact with
one Frame, the others remain on-screen. Figure 15.1 shows a typi-
cal page with three Frames, a large center **pane** and a **navigational frame** on the right, each with its own scrollbar, and a
third frame at the bottom displaying an advertisement.

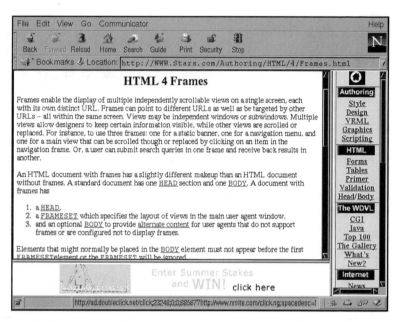

FIGURE 15.1 Frames.

BASIC FRAMES HTML MARKUP

As you've probably guessed, HTML uses a new tag to create Frames; it's called **<FRAMESET>**. Use <FRAMESET> within an ordinary HTML document to define a Frame to be called by that document. Let's look at the steps for creating an HTML document with Frames, and then consider each one.

- Define the number, orientation, and size of each Frame to be created.

- Specify URLs for the documents that are to be displayed in each of your Frames.

- Create the HTML documents to be displayed within your Frames.

DEFINING FRAMES

You need to specify the number, orientation, and size of your Frames. Do this with one of two <FRAMESET> attributes, **COLS** (for vertical Frame dividers) and **ROWS** (for horizontal dividers). Here's an example fragment that creates two Frames, oriented vertically, each using half the browser window.

> **<FRAMESET COLS="50/,50/">**

You can also specify absolute values in pixels for COLS and ROWS, rather than percentages of the window as we've done here. Using absolute values allows you to size a frame to fit an in-line image, for example. To do so, leave off the trailing slashes shown for each value. Whether you're using relative or absolute values, the number of values you enter here defines the number of Frame divisions.

> **One Hundred Percent Faithful**   Naturally, in using relative values for your Frame sizes, the total cannot exceed 100 percent.

SPECIFY URLS

Let's add two URLs to the preceding fragment, and also wrap basic HTML housekeeping markup around it to complete the document:

> **<HTML><HEAD><TITLE>First Frame Document </TITLE></HEAD>**
>
> **<FRAMESET COLS="50/,50/">**
>
> **<FRAME SRC="frame1.htm">**
>
> **<FRAME SRC="frame2.htm">**
>
> **</FRAMESET></HTML>**

Here, we've specified a couple of local documents, *frame1.htm* and *frame2.htm*, as the source for what's to appear in our Frames. Your Frames markup won't work, of course, until you create these documents. You can also use a full URL here, if your document resides elsewhere. Note also the closing **</FRAMESET>** tag.

> **Corpus Delecti?** Notice there's no <BODY> tag in the example. This is OK, as the <FRAMESET> tag substitutes for <BODY>. See the section "Supporting Non-Frames Browsers" later in this lesson for an exception to this rule.

CREATE DOCUMENTS

It's important to note this example document contains no substantive material, just references to *other* documents. Before your Frames document is ready to be viewed, of course, you need to create the two other, separate HTML documents to be called by it. Here's *frame1.htm*:

> **<HTML><HEAD><TITLE>Left Frame</TITLE>**
> **</HEAD><BODY><H1>This is the Left Frame</H1>**
>
> **Click within this frame to make it active.**
> **</BODY></HTML>**

As you can see, this is simple HTML. Here's *frame2.htm*, which is slightly more complex, but still nothing you haven't already seen:

> **<HTML><HEAD><TITLE>Right Frame</TITLE>**
> **</HEAD><BODY><H1>This is the Right Frame</H1>**
>
> **<IMG ALT="[Explorer Logo]" ALIGN="LEFT"**
> **SRC="ie.gif">Frame documents are ordinary HTML**
> **documents, and they can contain anything an**
> **HTML document can, including inline images and**
> **regular <A HREF="foo.htm">hyperlinks</A>.**
> **</BODY></HTML>**

Figure 15.2 shows our first Frames document.

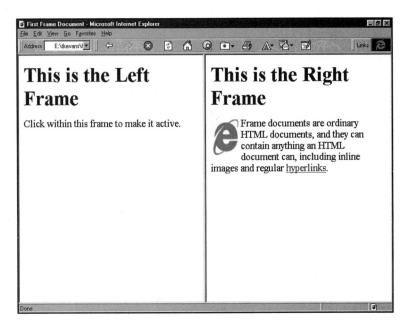

FIGURE 15.2   Basic Frames document.

ADVANCED FRAMES HTML MARKUP

As you can see from Figure 15.1, you can divide your window into more than two frames. Create multiple frames by nesting one set of <FRAMESET> tags inside another. Here's a short example introducing nested <FRAMESET> tags.

```
<HTML><HEAD><TITLE>Home</TITLE>
</HEAD><FRAMESET COLS="30/,70/">

<FRAMESET ROWS="80/,20/">

<FRAME SRC="framelinks.html">

<FRAME SRC="framenav.html"
SCROLLING="auto"></FRAMESET>
```

```
<FRAME SRC="http://home.netscape.com"
NAME="right"></FRAMESET></HTML>
```

It's easier for you to interpret this if you look at Figure 15.3.

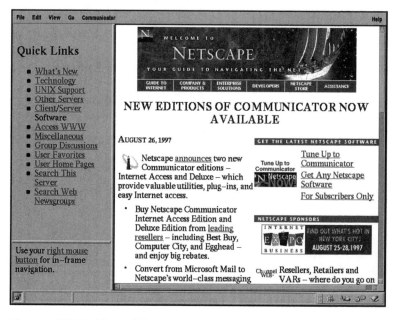

FIGURE 15.3   Nested Frames.

The second <FRAMESET> tag divides the left frame in two, splitting it 80/20 horizontally (using the ROWS attribute). Each <FRAME> tag has an HTML document as its source. The example, loading two local files and one URL (the Netscape Home Page), shows how you can create custom Web pages with Frames that incorporate remote sites. Note the use of the SCROLLING attribute for the navigational frame; if the browser is resized, a scrollbar will appear automatically.

Frames has a nifty capability of letting hyperlinks in one frame load documents in a *different* frame. You may have noticed the **NAME="right"** markup in the last line of our example. Here's just a couple of lines from the HTML document for the upper-left frame, *framelinks.html*, which uses it:

<H1>Quick Links</H1>

<UL><LI><A HREF="http://home.netscape.com/ home/whats-new.html" TARGET="right">What's New</A></LI>

As you can see, this line also contains the *right* value to the **TARGET** attribute. The relationship between this label in the two HTML documents allows a link clicked in the upper-left window to be loaded into the *right* window. The two left frames stay in place, while the new document, Netscape's *What's New* page in this case, gets loaded in the right window.

IN-LINE FRAMES NEW IN HTML 4.0

HTML 4.0 adds a new feature, called **in-line** Frames, which allows you to pop a frame in the middle of an otherwise standard HTML document. Thus, rather than dividing your entire browser window into horizontal or vertical frames, you can actually display a single frame as an independent document within a Web page. Here's example markup creating an in-line frame:

<HTML><HEAD><TITLE>In-line Frame</TITLE> </HEAD><BODY>

<H1>In-Line Frames</H1>

So far, this document is an ordinary, non-frames HTML page, containing standard HTML markup. Below, however, you can see an <EM>in-line </EM>frame.

<P ><IFRAME SRC="tkevans.html" WIDTH="700" HEIGHT="200" SCROLLING="auto" FRAMEBORDER="1"></IFRAME>

<H1>Document Resumes Here</H1>

**After the <EM>in-line</EM> frame, the standard
HTML markup resumes.</BODY></HTML>**

Figure 15.4 shows a document containing an in-line Frame. As to
the specifics of the markup:

- The frame, which is in fact another document (or URL), is
  sized in absolute pixels using the **WIDTH** and **HEIGHT**
  attributes.

- A scrollbar is added using the **SCROLLING** attribute (the
  auto value means the scrollbar appears if the document
  is larger than the frame in which it appears).

- A frame border is added, using the Boolean attribute
  FRAMEBORDER; setting the value to 0 (zero) instead of
  1 (one) suppresses the border.

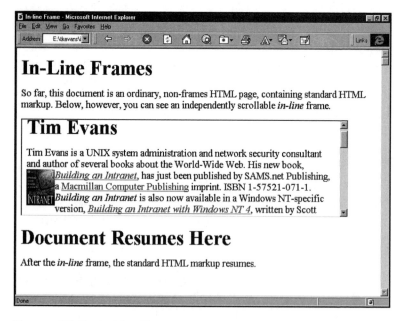

FIGURE 15.4   In-Line Frame

As you can also see, the in-line Frame is a fully functional HTML document, containing an in-line image and clickable hyperlinks.

FRAMES NAVIGATION

There's a non-intuitiveness about navigation in Frames which you need to know. Normally, users click the **Back** and **Forward** buttons in their Web browser to navigate previous Web pages they've visited. When you're interacting with Frames pages, however, clicking Back/Forward doesn't do what users have come to expect.

If you want to backtrack within a Frames document instead of clicking Back, use your **right mouse button** while in the frame you want to leave. Doing so will generate a pop-up within the frame, with both **Back** and **Forward** selections. As you move through Frames, this pop-up menu allows you to move in the way you're accustomed to moving with the Back and Forward buttons.

SUPPORTING NON-FRAMES BROWSERS

As you learned in Lesson 11, "Adding Images to Your Document," providing alternative text allows your pages to support browsers which don't do images and also allows for the appropriate display of pages when users turn off image loading. HTML 4.0 provides similar support for Frames features.

You'll recall the <FRAMESET> tag replaces <BODY> in an HTML document with Frames. To make sure everyone can view your documents, though, you can go ahead and include an ordinary <BODY> section in your pages, right along with your Frames markup. Under HTML 4.0 standards, browsers that don't understand Frames markup will simply skip the Frames markup and zero in on <BODY>, which they do understand. Similarly, if a user has turned off Frames support in his browser, the rest of the page will be displayed. Here's what this looks like:

<HTML><HEAD><TITLE>Frames. No Frames </TITLE></HEAD>

```
<FRAMESET COLS="50/,50/">
...frames markup...</FRAMESET>
<BODY>
...ordinary HTML page...</BODY></HTML>
```

HTML 4.0 adds the **<NOFRAMES>** tag to further clarify this situation. You've no doubt seen Frames pages on the Web which contain a table of contents for a document in one Frame and the text of the document in another. You can craft your HTML to ensure it's viewable both in Frames and non-Frames versions, without having to write the document twice. Here's how:

- Create an HTML page, called *body.html*, containing the body of your document and the <NOFRAMES> tag, like this:

```
<HTML><BODY><NOFRAMES>
...table of contents here...</NOFRAMES>
...literal body of document...</BODY></HTML>
```

- Create a table of contents document named *toc.html*
- Create a Frames reference page, *frametop.html*, for your document, like this:

```
<HTML><FRAMESET COLS="50/,50/">
<FRAME SRC="body.html"">
<FRAME SRC="toc.html"></FRAMESET>
<BODY>You may want to look at a <a
href="body.html">non-Frames version</a> of this
document.</BODY></HTML>
```

Browsers that load *frametop.html* will render it as follows:

- Frames-savvy browsers will display your two documents (*toc.html* and *body.html*) in the normal, Frames manner. The browser ignores the <NOFRAMES> tag, preventing downloading the documents twice.

- Browsers that don't support Frames will be prompted to load the non-Frames version of the page, which is actually your *body.html* document, containing both the table of contents and the body of the document.

I Meant What I Said   <NOFRAMES> doesn't mean the document has no Frames markup; browsers without Frames capabilities don't know about <NOFRAMES>. Instead, <NOFRAMES> instructs a Frames-capable browser to *suppress* Frames rendering. This is a little tricky in our example, so let's restate what happens. Your two documents are displayed (in Frames) by the browser. The left frame shows your Table of Contents (*toc.html*), while inside your right frame (*body.html*), the portion of the document marked off with <NOFRAMES> is **not** displayed, since it's already displayed in the left frame. In the right Frame, only the body of your document appears.

Love, Hate, and Frames   People either love Frames, thinking they're the coolest thing since UNIX, or they hate them. It's not just the fact the **Back** button no longer works as they're used to it working, it's also that the whole browser history mechanism (accessed from the **Go** pulldown) is whopperjaw and they lose their place easily. This sort of frustration for HTML authors to provide alternative content, supporting Frames-impaired browsers and giving users the choice of non-Frames pages, either with an explicit top-level page choice or with markup using <NOFRAMES>.

In this lesson, you've learned about adding snappy-looking Frames to your Web pages. The capabilities of Frames seem quite attractive, but users have found problems navigating them. In the next lesson, we'll return to HTML 4.0 Style Sheets, using them to add color to your Web pages.

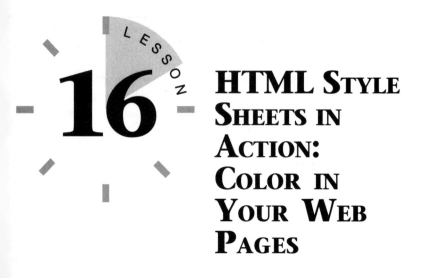

HTML STYLE SHEETS IN ACTION: COLOR IN YOUR WEB PAGES

In this lesson, you'll learn more about HTML style sheets, using them to add color in your HTML documents. Even if adding color seems unimportant to you, this lesson uses it as an example of the wider application of style sheets in HTML 4.0.

WIDE APPLICATION OF STYLE SHEETS IN HTML 4.0

Style sheets are probably the most fundamental change in HTML 4.0. As you learned in Lesson 5, "Introduction to HTML Style Sheets," they are, in fact, pervasive, applying to all elements of the language. HTML tags and other elements can be used in combination with style sheets to enhance your Web pages and simplify your life as an HTML author. Several other lessons have given you examples of style sheet markup, but you've not seen a formal discussion of its fundamentals. Let's do that now, but in the context of adding color.

BASIC CONCEPTS OF STYLE SHEETS

HTML 4.0 styles are implemented using style sheet **rules**. All rules consist of two parts, a **selector** and a **declaration**. Here's an example you learned earlier for setting a font size and font type for headlines:

H1 { font-size: 18pt; font-style: italic }

In this example, **H1** is your selector, while the material within the **curly braces** forms the declaration.

> **! No Brackets**   The angle brackets normally used with HTML tags are not used in style sheet selectors.

Declarations are also divided in two, including one or more **properties** and their corresponding **values**. Within the example declaration, two properties, *font-size* and *font-style*, are specified, each with a value. Note the two property-value pairs are separated by a semicolon, while the pairs themselves use a colon separator.

As with the HTML 4.0 standard itself, you can read detailed information on style sheets at the World Wide Web Consortium's Web site, **http://www.w3.org/**. See in particular **http://www.w3.org/TR/REC-CSS1** for detailed specifics, from which much of the style sheets material in this *10 Minute Guide* was adapted.

Color on Your Web Pages Using Style Sheets

Let's explore style sheets by seeing how they can be used to set text and background colors in your Web pages. Bear in mind throughout this lesson, what you're learning about style sheets applies across the board in HTML 4.0, not just to color. We've selected color to illustrate style sheets since it's both simple and of wide interest.

> **TIP   It's the Latest Style**   Style sheet rules can be applied to all HTML 4.0 tags.

In Lesson 6, "Creating Headlines, Typeface Styles, and Paragraphs," the subject of adding color to your Web pages using HTML 4.0 style sheets was introduced. There, you learned the basics of controlling the on-screen color of the text in your documents. Let's now add to this knowledge.

In HTML 4.0, all aspects of color are controlled using style sheets. Even though older HTML markup for setting colors (the **bgcolor** attribute, for example) may still work in today's new Web browsers, you'll want to take advantage of style sheets instead since they're both easier and more flexible.

OVERALL BACKGROUND AND TEXT COLORS

To specify overall background and text colors for an HTML page, use the **<STYLE>** tag within the <HEAD> portion of the document. Here's an example, creating an HTML document with a white background and red text:

> **<HEAD><STYLE TYPE="text/css"**
>
> **BODY { color: red; background: white }**
>
> **</STYLE></HEAD>**

Besides using the 16 standard colors you learned in Lesson 6, you can also use hexadecimal RGB triplets to express color selections. In our previous example, substitute "FFFFFF" for "white" and "FF0000" for "red." (Refer to Lesson 6 for specifics on RGB triplets.)

TIP   **Cool Green**   The author, being an amateur actor, often uses a just barely noticeable, cool green background color (the color of pre-performance-calming Green Rooms) to soothe the savage Web browser. Try a background color of "EEFFFA."

Colors Out of Whack?   You'll recall our discussion of how different computer hardware affects the rendering of your Web pages. Color is especially sensitive to users' video cards and monitors. Low-end, low-resolution cards and monitors won't give true color in all cases and, of course, monochrome monitors don't give any colors at all. Be sure to test-view your HTML documents that use color on as many different systems as you can to get an idea of how your color selections actually get displayed. You may have to stick with less-subtle colors.

Multiple Style Sheet Rules

You can put as many style sheet rules in a document as you want. Suppose, for example, you want all the headlines in your document to appear in colors different from the rest of the text, and that level-1 and level-2 headlines should be in different colors from each other. Let's extend our previous example:

> **<HEAD><STYLE TYPE="text/css"**
>
> **BODY { color: red; background: white }**
>
> **H1 { color: green }**
>
> **H2 { color: 000000 }**
>
> **</STYLE></HEAD>**

Here, we've set level-1 headlines to appear in green text, and level-2 headlines in black. (Note the use of the hexidecimal expression of the color black, showing you can mix color names and hex descriptions.)

> **TIP**
>
> **Scotch Doubles**   You might have guessed style sheet rules don't have to be limited to a single subject, such as color. Recall our earlier headline example, setting font size and font type. To add it to your color specification, change the earlier H1 rule to read:
>
> **H1 { color: green; font-size: 18pt; font-style: italic }**

CHANGING COLORS WITHIN YOUR DOCUMENTS

Style sheet rules within the <HEAD> section of an HTML document are called **embedded** style sheets. Embedded style sheets control the overall document. Setting your background and text colors in this way, for example, applies across the board in the document. In addition, as you learned in Lesson 6, you can apply **in-line** styles to *individual* HTML tags and sections of a document. You learned to change the text color of a *single paragraph within a document* with markup like this:

<P COLOR="blue">Text of a paragraph that appears in blue type.</P>

> **!**
>
> **Tan (Shoes) and Pink (Shoelaces)?**   Watch the combinations of your text and background colors. A potential problem, besides garish color contrasts, is a combination in which your text disappears into the background color because there's not enough contrast between the two colors. As with your images, be sure to view your pages with colors on as many different computer screens as you can, so you can see how different hardware renders your colors.
>
> Remember, in particular, to select contrasting colors, so viewers with monochrome monitors won't find your documents difficult to read.

Controlled by this in-line style sheet rule, your paragraph displays in blue type, while all the other text in the document appears in the color you selected with your overall, embedded style sheet rules.

STILL MORE COLOR

You can create a dramatic effect by using a contrasting background for particular HTML tags. Here's our example markup revised and extended to use a new style sheet property, **background color**:

> **<HEAD><STYLE TYPE="text/css"**
>
> **BODY { color: red; background: white }**
>
> **H1 { color: white; background-color: red}**
>
> **H2 { color: green; background-color: pink}**
>
> **</STYLE></HEAD>**

While these may turn out to be poor color combinations, and Figure 16.1 doesn't show the actual colors, you can see how this markup is rendered in Internet Explorer 4.0.

PRECEDENCE OF STYLE SHEET RULES

As you might have surmised from the last example, using an in-line style sheet rule allows you to override an embedded style sheet rule since it applies only to a section of a document. This seems logical if you think about it. Embedded style sheet rules, like nearly all rules, allow exceptions in the form of in-line rules.

As you'll learn in Lesson 19, "Cascading Style Sheets," there's a formal hierarchy of precedence among style sheet rule types. For the time being, though, use this rule of thumb: **The more specific the style sheet rule, the higher its precedence.**

Selecting a color for an individual paragraph or headline with an in-line style sheet rule, for example, overrides colors selected in your embedded rules. Of course, where there is no overall style sheet rule for a given HTML element, your in-line rules apply, but only to the portion of the document in which you've used it.

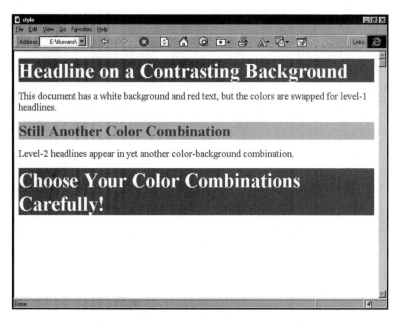

FIGURE 16.1   Headlines on contrasting background.

STYLE SHEETS THAT APPLY TO A GROUP OF DOCUMENTS

There's one more kind of style sheet rule you haven't learned yet. If you can make style sheet rules that apply across the board in a *document*, you might wonder whether you can have rules that apply to *all of your documents*. After all, this seems the logical extension of the style-sheet principle.

In fact, HTML 4.0 does provide just such a mechanism, called **linked** style sheets. You can create a separate, **master** style document, containing HTML markup for all your rules, which you then link into individual HTML documents. All the style definitions in your master style sheet are carried over into all HTML documents containing links to it. Making a change in the master document applies to all documents that link to it.

Whether you used linked or embedded style sheets to set out the general properties (like colors) of your documents depends on how extensive your rules are. If all your rules do is set a couple of colors, there's probably little gain from using linked style sheets, but if you have an extensive list of rules, it's a major productivity improvement, particularly since you can apply rules changes to many documents all at once by just changing the master style sheet.

Finding Colors

In Lesson 6, you learned how to use your calculator or the Windows 95 Paint program to convert colors into the hexadecimal numbers used here. You can find a nifty, clickable color palette (shown in Figure 16.2) on the Web at **http://www. hidaho.com/colorcenter/cc.html**. Clicking a color shows its hexadecimal equivalents. In addition, you'll actually see the on-screen background and text change as you test colors. (This page, incidentally, uses Frames and is powered by Java, about which you'll learn in Lesson 17, "Active Web Pages with Java and ActiveX.")

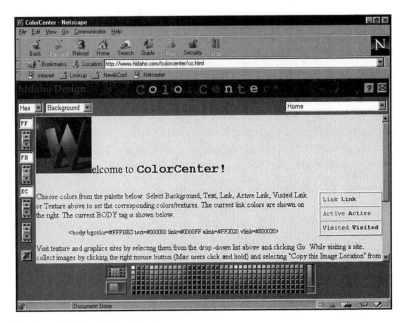

FIGURE 16.2   Color Center.

> **For UNIX Users Only** While most modern UNIX systems
> **TIP** include a graphical *calctool* which can do decimal-hex
> conversions, UNIX users can also use the command-line
> *bc* utility to do quick conversions for colors. Here's an
> example, shown with the standard dollar sign UNIX shell
> prompt:
>
> **$ bc**
>
> **ibase=10**
>
> **obase=16**
>
> **158 * 1**
>
> **9E**
>
> **...**
>
> **<CTRL-D>**
>
> **$**
>
> As you can see, the *ibase* and *obase* commands within
> *bc* set the input and output base (decimal and hex, re-
> spectively). Simply multiply any decimal number by 1 to
> get its hex equivalent. Continue doing such multiplica-
> tions until you have all your hex numbers. As with most
> UNIX utilities, pressing **Ctrl+D** exits *bc*.

In this lesson, you learned more about HTML 4.0 style sheets, using them to put colors in your HTML documents. We'll return to style sheets for one final pass in Lesson 19. In the next lesson, though, we'll turn to Active Web pages.

ACTIVE WEB PAGES WITH JAVA AND ACTIVEX

In this lesson, you'll learn about making your Web pages active with Java applets and ActiveX controls.

Computer industry pundits have hailed HTML 4.0's integration of the competing Java and ActiveX technologies into a single framework as a major step forward. Let's take a look at these two, and you can decide for yourself whether this is in fact true.

WHAT ARE JAVA AND ACTIVEX?

Sun Microsystems' Java, now seemingly licensed by anyone who has anything to do with computers, has been the first real breakthrough in Web interactivity since CGI scripting. ActiveX, however, is neck and neck with Java for creating active Web pages. Let's look at the two, which are in some respects similar.

JAVA

Java **applets**, as they're called, are computer programs called from HTML documents. Applets are downloaded from a Web server, then run on the user's computer. The success of Java is based on Java applets being completely platform-independent. That is, the exact same Java applet will run just as well on your PC or Macintosh as it does on a Sun, IBM, Silicon Graphics, or Hewlett-Packard workstation running UNIX.

This sort of platform independence has been the Holy Grail of computing since the second computer was invented. Software vendors now have the opportunity to sell their products, and

have them run, right out of the box, on just about every computer around, without their having to go to the time, trouble, and
expense of porting it. Once Netscape and Microsoft added Java
support to their Web browsers, a huge Java frenzy developed.

Any Port in a Storm   Most large computer programs are
compiled into machine-readable code. Each kind of
computer—PCs, Macs, and every different UNIX
system—require a separate compilation. In most cases,
the underlying **source code** needs modification, called
porting, for each different computer hardware and operating system before compilation. The differences between
these platforms are so significant and porting is often
either impossible or too expensive to consider, so vendors often limit themselves and their products to one
platform.

ACTIVEX

ActiveX is a means by which a wide range of PC programs can be
called from HTML documents. ActiveX **controls** are downloaded
from a Web server, then the PC programs they control are run on
the user's PC. Unlike Java applets, ActiveX controls are, so far,
limited to PCs running Windows 95/NT and, just lately, Macs
running Internet Explorer version 4. Figure 17.1 shows an example of an ActiveX control.

Once and Future King?   Microsoft has promised UNIX
support for ActiveX (and an accompanying port of
Internet Explorer) for the first quarter of 1998—long after
its initial target date of late 1996.

FIGURE 17.1   ActiveX control.

HOW JAVA AND ACTIVEX WORK

As we've noted, Java applets and ActiveX controls are similar in that they're downloaded by Web browsers, then run on the user's own computer. Let's look at a little of how each works.

JAVA

Java applets are written in the Java programming language, then compiled into platform-independent **byte code**. Somewhere between ordinary plain-text program source code and binary machine language code, Java-compatible Web browsers read the incoming Java byte codes and execute the applets they represent on the user's computer. Java applets, then, are a lot like Helper applications or plug-ins, except you download them just as you need them, instead of beforehand. Java applets can be full-featured, fully interactive programs.

Figure 17.2 shows a Java application, which calculates the best route between any two stations in the New York subway system. Check this out at **http://www.transarc.com/afs/ transarc.com/public/brail/html/transit/nycall.html**.

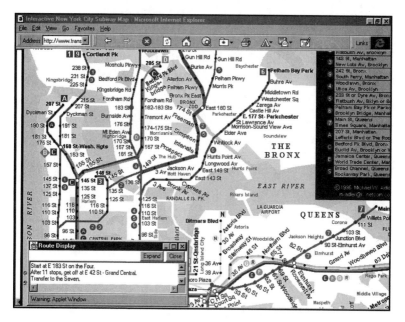

FIGURE 17.2   New York subway system routing Java applet.

Vendors are announcing Java-based products right and left, while Java development software (that is, tools software developers can use to create Java applets) is everywhere. Sun's own Java Development Kit is available at no cost, for Sun's Solaris (UNIX), running on both Sparc and x86 (Intel) CPUs, Windows NT and Windows 95, and the Macintosh, at **http://www. javasoft.com/**.

Java Programming Language   Java is a full-blown, object-oriented programming language that has been expressly engineered for use on the World Wide Web. You'll need a significant programming background to learn it.

ACTIVEX

ActiveX is based on an extended and renamed Microsoft technology once called **Object Linking and Embedding**, or **OLE**; it's now called **Component Object Module**, or **COM**.

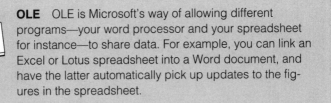

OLE   OLE is Microsoft's way of allowing different programs—your word processor and your spreadsheet for instance—to share data. For example, you can link an Excel or Lotus spreadsheet into a Word document, and have the latter automatically pick up updates to the figures in the spreadsheet.

COM shares many features of OLE, but adds support for Internet/ Web connectivity and multimedia. Internet Explorer implements ActiveX controls, allowing communication between the Web browser and a wide range of PC programs. Explorer dynamically downloads needed software when it encounters HTML documents calling **ActiveX controls**, then runs the downloaded software on your PC.

If this sounds a lot like Java applets to you, you're right.

THE <OBJECT> TAG: HTML PEACE?

Although Java and ActiveX programming are beyond the scope of this *10 Minute Guide*, the HTML markup used to make Web pages

interactive with them is not. Including ActiveX controls or Java
applets in your HTML documents is quite simple, and it's been
unified with the HTML 4.0 standard.

<OBJECT> BASICS

HTML 4.0 has broadly redefined the **<OBJECT>** tag, which was
previously used just with ActiveX controls. With the redefinition,
<OBJECT> is a high-level abstraction that deals with the **inclu-
sion** of things called **objects** in Web pages. Objects can be images, multimedia files, and even other HTML documents. More
importantly for this lesson, the new abstraction includes both
ActiveX controls and Java applets.

> **Applets and Objects**   HTML 4.0 now deprecates use
> of the <APPLET> tag for Java applets. Instead, use
> <OBJECT>.

A full discussion of <OBJECT> is inappropriate for this *10 Minute
Guide*, but we can look at its use with Java and ActiveX. The basic
idea is an included object is defined using various attributes of the
<OBJECT> tag. Let's introduce four of them most often used with
<OBJECT> in dealing with Java and ActiveX:

- **CLASSID** specifies an agent that will render the object;
  expressed as an URL

- **CODETYPE** defines the data type of an object

- **DATA** the actual Java or ActiveX object; also expressed as
  an URL

- **CODEBASE** points to the location where the objects
  physically live, also an URL

HTML MARKUP USING <OBJECT>

Here's an HTML fragment for a Java object, using some of these attributes:

> **<OBJECT CODETYPE="application/octet-stream"**
>
> **CODEBASE="http://www.mycompany.com/ java_apps"> CLASSID="java:my.java.class">**
> **</OBJECT>**

You'll recognize the value of the CODETYPE attribute, **application/octet-stream** as being in MIME format (see Lesson 13, "Helper Applications and Plug-Ins for Multimedia"); use this as boilerplate for all Java objects. As you can probably guess, the CLASSID attribute's value is simply the name of the Java applet that's being called. Notice, also, you're allowed to use a special **java** URL type as part of CLASSID. Finally, CODEBASE is an URL that specifies the directory in which the Java object will be found, allowing shorter URLs as CLASSID values.

For an ActiveX object, your HTML markup will look something like this:

> **<OBJECT CLASSID="clsid:12345abc-1xy7-22cf-a2bd-010045X56789"**
>
> **CODEBASE="http://www.mycompany.com/ activex/"> DATA=" my.activex.app"></OBJECT>**

Here, you can see the DATA attribute has the name of your ActiveX object as its value, while CODEBASE defines the location where the object can be found. The value of CLASSID is in URL format, with the new URL type **clsid**, followed by what appears to be a random batch of numbers and letters. In fact, this URL is the guaranteed-to-be-unique address of the object on the World Wide Web.

To summarize this whirlwind look at <OBJECT>:

- Two new URL types, *java* and *clsid* are allowed as values to the CLASSID attribute.

- CODEBASE specifies the location of the objects.
- DATA specifies the actual ActiveX object.
- CODETYPE specifies the kind of data, in MIME format.

MORE <OBJECT> ATTRIBUTES

The <OBJECT> tag has a number of other attributes that might interest you. Probably, the most important are **ALIGN, HEIGHT, WIDTH**, and **ALT**. Since Java and ActiveX objects often appear within your Web browser window or open new windows, these attributes give you control over where your applets appear on the screen and how large they are. All work like the image attributes you learned in Lesson 11, "Adding Images to Your Document."

PEACE?

As we've noted, the new <OBJECT> framework in HTML 4.0, incorporating both Java applets and ActiveX controls, has been hailed by some as some sort of peace treaty between Sun and Microsoft. While high-level abstractions of this sort, with massive sets of subdivisions, no doubt warm the hearts of techno-geeks, you may not find it so heartwarming. In fact, as you've seen, the <OBJECT> framework, extended to accommodate not only Java and ActiveX, but also nearly everything else you can throw into a Web page, is now so massive it may make your life as an HTML author more complex.

SECURITY WITH JAVA AND ACTIVEX

As you'll recall, active Web pages run Java or ActiveX programs right on your own computer. If you think about it, the whole idea of running a random program you find on some Web page on your computer is—or should be—a scary one. Clicking Web hyperlinks is so easy many people don't stop to think about the implications of what a rogue program might do to their PC. It's a sad fact of Internet life that there are people out there who get some sort of satisfaction out of damaging or destroying others' data, or of cracking into other people's computer systems to steal information.

A number of security problems have turned up in Java. While Sun has addressed these problems quickly, as have Web browser manufacturers such as Netscape, Java is a new language that may have undiscovered flaws that might be used by unscrupulous people to compromise the security of systems using innocuous-looking Java applets. You can read more about Java security in the World Wide Web Security FAQ at **http://www-genome.wi. mit.edu/WWW/faqs/www-security-faq.html**.

To deal with security in ActiveX, Microsoft has built into ActiveX a feature for using **verifiable digital signatures**. A vendor of ActiveX controls can include a digital certificate of authenticity and verifification the code hasn't been tampered with. Explorer, which has several "levels" of security you can select, will display these certificates and prompt the user for confirmation before continuing. Similarly, Explorer will confirm all downloads and pop up alerts, based on the security level you select, where ActiveX controls don't have such certificates.

Of course, there's nothing to keep a cracker from obtaining a valid certificate for a destructive ActiveX control, so you need to exercise the same caution as you would with any other unknown program. You can read more about ActiveX security in the World Wide Web Security FAQ.

JAVA OR ACTIVEX?

Java and ActiveX are in many respects competing technologies. Deciding whether to use one or the other in your Web pages is a difficult choice. You already know Java's biggest plus is its platform independence. If you expect your Web pages to be viewed by users with anything other than Internet Explorer, you'll want to stick to Java.

Plug Ncompass In   You can find information about a Netscape Plug-in that adds ActiveX support at **http://www.ncompass.com/**.

Because ActiveX builds on and extends OLE, your investment in PC hardware, software, and user training can be leveraged. While ActiveX isn't yet supported on Windows 3.*x*, it is on Windows 95/NT and Macintosh. With millions of these seats having shipped in the past couple of years, you can see how the integration of ActiveX and Internet Explorer can give you a jump start.

Paradoxically, this integration with current desktops is a potentially serious limitation to ActiveX. Web pages with ActiveX controls won't work on other platforms—the primary advantage of Java. Microsoft has, as noted earlier, promised a UNIX port of Internet Explorer, together with support for ActiveX, but it remains to be seen whether this will actually happen, and, if so, how well this software will be kept in step with the company's meat and potatoes PC platforms.

Your alternative is to develop CGI-driven Web pages that dynamically determine the browser type on each transaction, so they can provide either Java or ActiveX controls as appropriate.

This lesson has introduced Java and ActiveX objects, and given you the basics of the HTML markup that includes them in Web pages. In the next lesson, you'll learn more about making Web pages interactive through the use of Web-page scripting.

18

SCRIPTING ON HTML PAGES

In this lesson, you'll learn about embedding scripts in HTML pages. Scripting is a relatively simple way to add interactivity to your Web pages, though you'll need some programming experience to make the most of it.

WHAT IS WEB PAGE SCRIPTING AND WHY DO I NEED IT?

Early implementations of the World Wide Web were inadequate for many people's needs and tastes. While you've learned how to author basic HTML documents with a lot of useful formatting tricks, and also learned about fill-in forms and CGI scripts, the Web pages you've created so far are, for the most part, static. They don't do much of anything other than sit there on your screen. You probably want your Web pages to be *interactive*.

Over the past couple of years, Web developers have come up with several ways of making Web pages more interactive and useful— something more than just on-screen reading material. You learned about Sun Microsystems' *Java*, as well as Microsoft's *ActiveX* in the last lesson. Both have much in common with Web-page scripting. Let's make a simple start with Web-page scripting, using Netscape's **JavaScript** and Microsoft Visual Basic Script, more often referred to as **VBScript**.

Figure 18.1 shows part of a Web page powered by JavaScript. It's an interactive currency converter. The user selects two currencies from the scrollable lists, then enters an amount in either currency box. The JavaScript program, running on the user's computer, calculates the conversion and pops it into the other box.

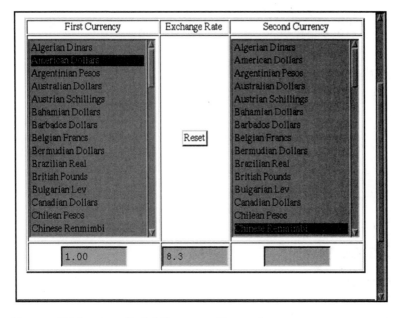

FIGURE 18.1 JavaScript Currency Converter.

What's in a Name? JavaScript began as Netscape's **LiveScript**. Almost immediately, as the Java craze hit, Netscape and Sun struck a naming deal and LiveScript became JavaScript. There's almost no real connection between Java and JavaScript, except for the similar, market-driven names.

Microsoft reverse-engineered JavaScript to produce its version, called **JScript**, for Internet Explorer, though IE is mostly JavaScript-compatible as well. This *10 Minute Guide* doesn't distinguish between JavaScript and JScript.

Use the Force   There's a critical distinction between CGI scripts and Web-page scripts. CGI scripts perform computations on the Web server, while, as noted with respect to Figure 18.1, Web-page scripts run *on the user's own computer*. The big gain from local processing is in speed and responsiveness. Rather than having to send data over the network (or over the Internet) to a remote Web server and wait for it to find time to do the currency conversion and return the results back across the network, the user's own computer does the work, almost instantaneously.

PROGRAMMING LANGUAGES

Web-page scripting languages are, in fact, programming languages. Let's look at some of their aspects.

INTERPRETED LANGUAGE

Web-page scripting languages are **interpreted**. This means scripts are read and executed line by line, just like old-fashioned **BASIC** or DOS batch files, and also like modern languages such as **perl**. Code is in plain text, and two simple, one-line scripts look like this:

> **document.write('Hello World
');**
>
> **MsgBox "Hello World!",0,"My first active document"**

The first example is in JavaScript, while the second is in VBScript. We won't go into the pros and cons of interpreted languages, or specific syntax, but you can probably guess what both of these do.

CODE GOES IN YOUR HTML DOCUMENTS

Web-page scripting code is not written in separate program files (although plans are to make this possible in the future). Rather, you include it right into your ordinary HTML documents. Let's wrap one of those Hello, World examples into a complete HTML document:

<HTML><HEAD><TITLE>VBScript Hello World </TITLE></HEAD>

<BODY><SCRIPT LANGUAGE="VBScript">

MsgBox "Hello World!",0,"My first active document"

</SCRIPT></BODY></HTML>

As you can see, we've used the **<SCRIPT>** tag and its **LAN-GUAGE** attribute. Figure 18.2 shows what it looks like when the HTML document is loaded in Internet Explorer. The pop-up box created by the **MsgBox** function is interactive, requiring a click on the OK button to make it go away. As you can see, simple scripting like this can be used to call users' attention to something, and require their acknowledgment of the alert.

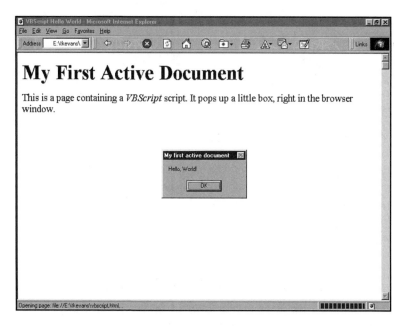

FIGURE 18.2   Hello World VBScript in Internet Explorer.

PORTABILITY OF WEB-PAGE SCRIPTS

Although we're treating JavaScript and VBScript as generic replacements in this lesson, you need to know a critical difference between them relating to their portability among different Web browsers.

- JavaScript programs are completely portable among many different kinds of computers. Netscape and other Web browsers have JavaScript capabilities built right in. Therefore, it doesn't matter if you're running Netscape on a Mac or UNIX system, or Internet Explorer on a PC; the script will run, since it's interpreted by your own browser, not the server.

- VBScript Web pages, on the other hand, are supported only in Internet Explorer. Netscape and most other Web browsers will not work with VBScript pages.

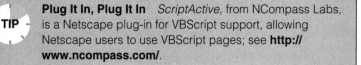

Plug It In, Plug It In   *ScriptActive*, from NCompass Labs, is a Netscape plug-in for VBScript support, allowing Netscape users to use VBScript pages; see **http://www.ncompass.com/**.

Another portability question lies with older browsers, such as *Mosaic* or *Lynx*, which don't support any kind of scripting. Since Web-page scripts are embedded right in HTML pages, it's possible for older Web browsers to get confused when they encounter scripts. While they'll normally just ignore the <SCRIPT> tag, multi-line scripts may still have unintended effects on an older browser. You need to hide your scripts, using HTML **comment markup**, from older Web browsers. Here's a JavaScript example:

```
<SCRIPT LANGUAGE="JavaScript">
<!--
document.write('<HR>Local time is ' + Date());
```

document.write('. <EM>What\'s New</EM> was last modified on ' + document.lastModified);

document.write('<HR>');

// -->

</SCRIPT>

We'll discuss this script further in the next section. In the meantime, note two kinds of comment markup being used here. The first is the standard HTML comment tags **<!--** and **-->**, marking the beginning and end of a multi-line comment. In addition, JavaScript's own internal comment marker, the double forward slash, **//**, is used within the script to hide the regular end-comment mark (**-->**) from the script itself. Older Web browsers will ignore the <SCRIPT> tag altogether and, since the rest of the script is inside HTML comment markers, it, too, will be ignored.

SCRIPTING AND BROWSER WINDOWS

In the VBScript "Hello, World" example previously (refer to Figure 18.2), the script opens a new window; JavaScript has similar capabilities. Both languages can be used not only for pop-up dialog boxes, but also can bring up whole new browser windows that display other Web pages, including ones dynamically created by the script itself.

Besides creating and manipulating new windows, Web-page scripts can also modify the display of the current HTML document. Figure 18.3 shows a Web page with the JavaScript example you just saw. Note the center of the page, where there are two *horizontal rules*, inside of which two sentences stating the current time and last-modification date of the page appear. There are several important things to note about this JavaScript example:

- The entire passage, beginning with the first horizontal rule and ending with the second one, is generated by the script.

- The script actually generates HTML markup by using the JavaScript **document.write( )** function. You can easily pick out the HTML markup that's created, including the horizontal rules (<HR>), and emphasized text (<EM>).

- The output of two other JavaScript functions, **Date( )** and **document.lastModified( )**, are integrated into the text of the passage.

- While the modification date on the document won't change unless the document is modified again, the current date and time are dynamically generated *each time the page is loaded* by reading the internal clock on the user's computer. This shows how scripts run on the user's own computer, not on a Web server somewhere. Date and time will be in the user's time zone, of course.

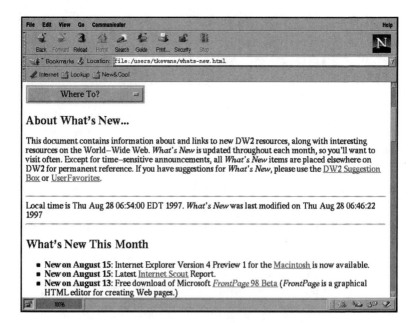

FIGURE 18.3 Web page with the JavaScript example.

MORE WEB-PAGE SCRIPT DEMOS

The *10 Minute Guide* format doesn't permit extensive technical discussion of the JavaScript and VBScript languages, but a couple of screenshots can show you more of what's possible. Check out Figure 18.4, which shows an interactive graphing tool. Just fill in figures in the on-screen boxes and get new bar graph's drawn instantly. Here you have a portable graphing tool—a poor man's Lotus 1-2-3—that works on your PC, your boss's Mac, and all the UNIX boxes in the Engineering Department. The URL for this Web site is **http://www.infohiway.com/javascript/**. You'll find many JavaScript examples there to download and play with.

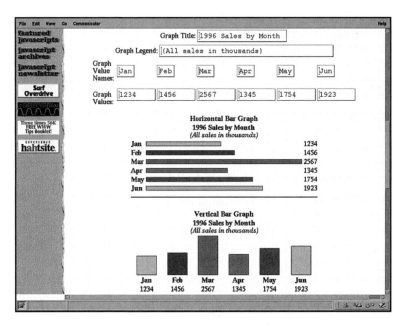

FIGURE 18.4 JavaScript automatic graphing.

Figure 18.5 illustrates a similar interactive charting tool written in VBScript. The URL for this Web site is **http://www.rollins-assoc.com/**.

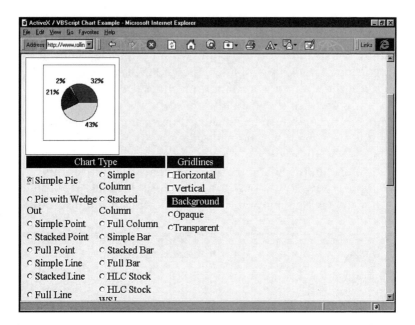

FIGURE 18.5   VBScript charting example.

CHOOSING A SCRIPTING LANGUAGE

Both JavaScript and VBScript are programming languages, and far more complex than HTML markup. If you have no programming experience, you might find VBScript somewhat easier to pick up than JavaScript. You can learn more about VBScript on the Web at **http://www.microsoft.com/vbscript/**. This page has links to more information and many more VBScript examples you can try out with your copy of Explorer. For JavaScript basics, see Netscape's DevEdge pages at **http://developer.netscape.com/ library/documentation/**.

VBScript's potential ease-of-learning, however, is offset by the fact that it's supported only by Internet Explorer. As with many other aspects of HTML, your choices here are dictated by the browsers used to access your pages. If everyone's using Explorer, by all means go ahead with VBScript. However, if Netscape comes into the picture, you'll need to consider JavaScript, since Explorer also supports JavaScript.

In this lesson, you learned about the Web-page scripting languages JavaScript and VBScript. Though the languages are different, their functions in HTML documents are similar, and both add interactivity to your Web pages. The next lesson will return to HTML 4.0 Style Sheets, focusing on rules of precedence, or Cascading.

19

CASCADING STYLE SHEETS

In this lesson about style sheets, you will learn how the various kinds of style sheet rules interact.

As you've learned, style sheets are a way of specifying overall characteristics of HTML documents. You've also learned there are several types of style sheet rules, but may not be clear about the relationship among them.

STYLE SHEET BASICS REVIEW

In earlier lessons in this 10 Minute Guide, you've learned a good deal about HTML 4.0 Style Sheets. Style sheets allow you to control most things in your Web pages, including indentation, margins, line leading, type point size, color, and just about everything else. While many ingenious HTML authors have devised workaround ways of doing these things in HTML, some of them are awkward and difficult to deal with. Style sheets make it simple.

Currently, no widely used Web browser other than Internet Explorer knows about style sheets. Browsers which don't support style sheets will simply ignore your style sheet markup. In addition, future HTML standards being considered will allow individual browser users to have **personal** style sheets that might well override those in your HTML documents.

You know there are three different kinds of style sheet usage:

- **In-line** style sheets
- **Embedded** style sheets
- **Linked** style sheets

Let's review these, then turn to **cascading style sheets**, in which rules of precedence among in-line, embedded, and linked style sheets are set.

IN-LINE STYLE MARKUP AFFECTS INDIVIDUAL HTML TAGS

Use in-line style markup to change the behavior of individual HTML tags:

> **<H1 STYLE="font-size: 18pt">This is My Large Headline</H1>**

Brackets, or Not?   You learned in Lesson 16 not to use angle brackets in *embedded* style sheet rules and to surround declarations with curly braces. *In-line* rules do require the angle brackets, but your declarations are enclosed in double quotes, rather than curly braces. To keep this straight in your mind, think of in-line style rules as tag-attribute pairs, much like those you already know.

You can specify multiple in-line declarations, like this:

> **<H1 STYLE="font-size: 18pt; font-style: italic; color: red">This is My Large Red Italic Headline</H1>**

Be sure to use the semicolon shown to separate multiple declarations in the same definition.

When you use in-line style markup like this, it applies only within the modified tag. In other words, having modified one of the headlines in an HTML document as shown in the previous example, all other headlines in the document would appear in their normal font size and style.

EMBEDDED STYLE SHEETS FOR INDIVIDUAL HTML PAGES

Embedded style sheets apply to an entire HTML document, and must appear within the <HEAD> portion of your document.

> **<HTML><HEAD><TITLE>Embedded Style Sheet </TITLE><STYLE TYPE="text/css">**
>
> **H1 { font-size: 18pt; font-style: italic } </STYLE> </HEAD><BODY>**

The example markup specifies you're using the HTML 4.0-standard cascading style sheets, a formal set of rules. As you've learned earlier, "<STYLE TYPE="text/css">" is basic HTML house-keeping; include it whenever you use embedded style sheets.

> **TIP**   **Any Tag** Style definitions can be applied to any HTML tag.

You can control multiple HTML elements using embedded style sheets, just by adding new style definitions.

> **<HTML><HEAD><TITLE>Embedded Style Sheet </TITLE><STYLE TYPE="text/css">**
>
> **H1 { font-size: 18pt; font-style: italic }**
>
> **BODY { background: aqua; color: FF0000; text-align: center } <STYLE></HEAD><BODY>**

New style definitions are simple to add; just add them inside other sets of curly braces. As you can see, red text on an aqua background is specified and all text in the document is to be centered on the page rather than left-aligned.

As noted earlier in the discussion of in-line style markup, you can override your embedded style sheet's definitions. For example, if you've defined your text color using an embedded style sheet as red, you can temporarily override it, say, for a single important paragraph, with in-line style markup. Just add the in-line markup at the point in your HTML document where you want the change to occur. Here's how:

<P STYLE="color: blue">Paragraph to appear in blue.</P>

Note the use of the quotes surrounding the STYLE declaration (instead of curly braces), as you'd expect with a tag-attribute pair.

LINKED STYLE SHEETS

Perhaps the most important advantage of HTML style sheets is they can be applied *across the board to a batch of HTML documents.* In this way, you can ensure your HTML documents have a common look and feel, based on your own style decisions. Further, you can make consistent style changes throughout all your documents simply by changing style definitions in a **master style sheet**.

A master style sheet is an overall style document, which you **link** into individual HTML documents. All the style definitions in your master style sheet are carried into all HTML documents containing links to it. The HTML markup to link to a master style sheet is quite simple:

<HEAD><TITLE>Linking Style Sheets</TITLE>

<LINK REL="STYLESHEET" HREF="http:// www.mycompany.com/ourstyle.css" TYPE="text/ css"></HEAD><BODY>

You see a couple of new HTML elements here, the **<LINK>** tag and its attribute **REL**. The latter creates a relationship to the <LINK> tag, and in this case, points to an external style sheet document. The <LINK> tag includes an URL of the actual document. Since this entire set of markup is within the <HEAD>

section of the document, the linked style sheet applies to everything in the HTML document.

The master style sheet document itself follows much the same
syntax as the embedded style sheet shown earlier in this lesson.
Just create a plain text file containing your style definitions, and
save it with the **.css** file name extension. You can override anything in your linked spreadsheet with either an embedded style
sheet or *in-line* markup within your individual document.

Figure 19.1 shows an example which uses all three kinds of style
markup. Here is the complete master style sheet for this document:

H1 { font-size: 48pt }

EM { color: gray }

The master style sheet contains nothing other than style sheet
selector-declaration pairs, one on each line. No other HTML
markup is needed.

The HTML code for the document itself follows:

<HTML><HEAD><TITLE>Stylesheet Demo</TITLE>

**<LINK REL="STYLESHEET" HREF="http://
www.mycom/mystyle.css" TYPE="text/css">**

<STYLE TYPE="text/css">

BODY { color: red; background: white }

</STYLE></HEAD><BODY>

**<H1 STYLE="font-size: 18pt; font-style: italic">
This is My Large Italic Headline</H1>**

**The above headline was set with a <EM>in-line
</EM> style tag. The page background is white,
with red text, as specified with an <EM>embedded
<EM> style rule.**

<H1>Biggest Headline</H1>

This headline was controlled by the <EM>linked </EM> master stylesheet, which calls for level-1 headlines in 48 point type and <EM>all emphasized text to appear in gray.</EM>

</BODY></HTML>

FIGURE 19.1   Style sheet examples.

CASCADING STYLE SHEETS

"Cascading Style Sheets" (**CSS**), is an unfortunate term, since it really isn't expressive of what it means. Throughout this lesson, we've dropped hints of what this is all about, but let's now focus on it.

In each of the three preceding sections, you've read in-line style markup, embedded style markup, and linked style sheets can be *mixed in the same HTML document.* You've probably wondered about conflicts among style definitions if two or more of these are mixed. CSS is a set of **precedence rules** that resolve any conflicting style definitions you might use. Here's a summary of CSS rules:

- In-line style markup has the highest precedence of any style definition, overriding conflicting style definitions in both linked and embedded style sheets.

- Style definitions in your embedded style sheets come next.

- In the absence of any embedded or in-line style markup, linked style sheets apply.

Put another way, style definitions in linked or embedded style sheets not overridden under a higher rule apply in your HTML documents. Thus, style sheet rules are said to **cascade**.

This means you can use linked style sheets for most all your styles' markup, and only use style definition *exceptions* within individual HTML pages. You don't need to copy an entire set of linked style sheet definitions into an embedded style sheet just to change a single definition. Instead, you just add the one exception, and let the rest of the linked style sheet continue to apply.

Let's look at how the style rules which created the example page shown in Figure 19.1 cascade:

- Our *master style* sheet specifies 48-point type for level-1 headlines, the use of gray text color for emphasized type; the second of the two headlines follows this rule.

- Our *embedded* style sheet rules call for document body background and text colors of white and red, respectively. Since there is no mention of background and text colors in the master style sheet, this rule applies across the board in the document. Further, because the embedded style sheet doesn't mention the <EM> tag, the master style sheet rule kicks in, calling for emphasized text to appear in gray.

- The in-line style rule calls for the first level-1 headline to appear in 18-point, italic type, overriding the master style sheet rule for level-1 headlines.

This summary allows us to restate the rule of thumb you learned in Lesson 16: **The more specific the style sheet rule, the higher its precedence.** Moreover, exceptions to more general style rules always apply, even when there is not a general rule.

FURTHER CASCADING RULES

Even with all these style sheets rules and their precedence, you also need to know Web browsers can be set up to override, or even ignore altogether, your style sheet rules. Internet Explorer, for instance, allows the user to explicitly turn off style sheets in the **Options/Advanced** dialog box. Web browsers come with default settings for font size, colors, and other items, which may not be the same as those your style sheets call for. Also, users can change these defaults in their browser Options/Preferences dialog boxes.

SO, WHERE DO STYLE SHEETS REALLY FIT IN?

Just about now, you're wondering where style sheets fit in this context—and possibly why you bothered to learn about them in the first place. HTML 4.0's CSS rules say a Web browser's own set of default font sizes, colors, and the like will override any conflicting style definitions in your HTML markup. This follows the rule of thumb stated previously.

Continuing the same rule of thumb, the CSS definition also allows for **personal style sheets** for users (that is, the results of users changing browser defaults) to override everything.

Why Bother, Then?

While it may seem frustrating to think your carefully crafted style sheet rules can just be ignored willy-nilly by users, if you think about it, you'll understand this fits in with overall aspects of using the World Wide Web. For instance, many users, as you'll recall, suppress the downloading of in-line images because they take too long to load over slow modem links. Does this mean you shouldn't use images in your Web pages? Of course not. Images add immeasurably to Web pages, and not using them just because a few users might not view them is not even a consideration.

Personal style sheets in Web browsers follow the same general principle of letting the browser user determine for himself how the browser will behave. Just as a user can choose not to load images, she can choose the font size and style that's most readable or attractive based on her personal preferences and needs. That some users can make this decision, however, shouldn't deter you from using style sheets, any more than you would be deterred from using in-line images; they're just too important not to use.

In this lesson, you've learned about cascading style sheets. In the next lesson, you'll turn to Dynamic HTML, where, among other things, you'll find style sheets popping up once again.

Introducing Dynamic HTML

In this lesson, you'll learn about Dynamic HTML, the latest competitive battleground in HTML, in which Netscape and Microsoft attempt to add further interactivity to Web pages.

You've learned in Lessons 17, "Active Web Pages with Java and ActiveX," and 18, "Scripting on HTML Pages," how you can make your Web pages interactive. **DHTML** is a new HTML capability that can further enhance your pages. Unfortunately, what Microsoft calls DHTML and what Netscape calls it are in fact widely divergent, with only a little in common. We'll look at what the two have in common first, then discuss the differences.

> **Not in the Standard** Neither Microsoft's nor Netscape's definitions of DHTML is included in the HTML 4.0 draft standard, though parts of them may be in the final standard.

What Is DHTML?

While DHTML means different things to Microsoft and Netscape, it can be very broadly defined for purposes of this *10 Minute Guide*. DHTML allows for Web pages to *change* after they've been loaded by a Web browser. Such changes can include, to list a few examples:

- Image animations or morphing
- Auto-reloading of pages, or changes in pages, after a set period of time has passed

- Actual changes in a page triggered by events such as user mouse movements

GENERIC DHTML

As noted, there is some commonality in the two versions of DHTML. Let's focus on them first, referring to the areas of commonality as **Generic DHTML.**

In other lessons, you've learned about HTML style sheets and the inclusion of objects (images, Java applets, ActiveX controls, and others) in Web pages. Generic DHTML provides for the extended use of style sheets to let you control the **placement of objects** on Web pages. Both Microsoft and Netscape support the W[3] draft on the positioning of HTML elements using style sheets (see **http://www.w3.org/TR/WD-positioning** for the current status of this draft). The basic idea is that objects can **float** atop a Web page, with their actual location controlled by DHTML markup.

> **It Floats**   Imagine laying a clear sheet of plastic on top of a Web page, making two **layers**. Objects, such as images, can be *floated* on the upper, transparent, layer. Using Generic DHTML, objects can be precisely placed by HTML authors, anywhere on the layer, even where they overlap what's in lower layers. (Later in this lesson, you'll learn about Netscape's new **<LAYER>** tag, which can accomplish the same thing.)

Use of generic DHTML for positioning objects requires that you conceptually break your HTML documents into three (or more) chunks:

- The **body** of the document, as signified by the **<BODY>** tag, containing everyday HTML markup

- An **outer** portion, defined in a style sheet, which has a specific positioning set

- One or more **inner** portions, also defined with style sheets

It helps to think of the inner and outer portions of a DHTML document as sheets of clear plastic laid on top the body of the document. On each of the plastic sheets (or layers), objects can be floated at locations independent of objects on the other layers. (Use of the names *inner* and *outer* isn't required; you can name them anything that makes sense to you, such as *layer1* and *layer2*.)

Let's look at some DHTML markup. First, define the characteristics of your outer and inner layers with an embedded style sheet (recall embedded style sheets must be within the **<HEAD>** section of your HTML document):

<STYLE TYPE="text/css">

#outer {position:absolute; top: 100px; left: 60px; width: 100px;}

#inner {position:absolute; top: 60px; left: 135px; width: 100px;}

</STYLE>

Here, two rectangular areas, both 100 screen pixels wide, are defined. They're placed at absolute positions on the two layers, using x-y pixel coordinates, which overlap. Now, let's use them to float two images in an HTML document, where you encounter a new HTML 4.0 tag, **<DIV>**:

<BODY><H1>Dynamic HTML--Outer Layer</H1>

<DIV ID="outer"><IMG ALT="outer layer image" SRC="image1.jpg"></DIV>

<DIV ID="inner">< MG ALT="inner layer image" SRC="image2.jpg"></DIV>

</BODY>

Earlier, you defined the inner and outer layers with an embedded style sheet. Here, the styles defined in them are applied to different parts of the document, as marked off with the **<DIV>** tags. <DIV> tags can include in-line style sheet markup, if that makes more sense to you. However you do it, your images float atop your HTML page, something like that shown in Figure 20.1.

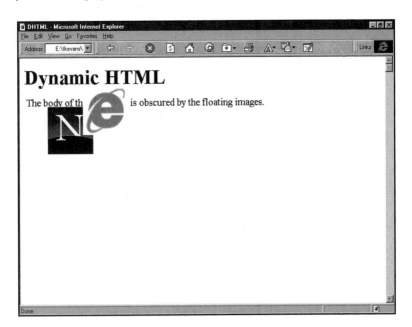

Figure 20.1   Floating, overlapping images.

Post No Bills   Notice how the text part of the <BODY> of the document is obscured by the floating, overlapping images. Of course, you'll ordinarily position your objects so they don't obscure other parts of your document, but this is a useful illustration.

Netscape's DHTML

Besides supporting the W³ draft on the positioning of HTML elements using style sheets, Netscape's conception of DHTML goes further in two respects:

- A separate means of floating objects atop Web pages, called **Layers**
- **Downloadable fonts**

Netscape Layers

Netscape supports a proprietary **<LAYER>** tag you can use for floating and positioning objects; <LAYER> is not supported by Internet Explorer. Here's our overlapping image page, rewritten using <LAYER>, with the resulting, almost identical, page shown in Figure 20.2:

> **<LAYER NAME="outer" LEFT="60" TOP="100" Z-INDEX="1">**
>
> **<IMG ALT="outer layer image" SRC="image1.jpg"></LAYER>**
>
> **<LAYER NAME="inner" LEFT="135" TOP="60" Z-INDEX="2">**
>
> **<IMG ALT="outer layer image" SRC="image1.jpg"></LAYER>**

Most of this should be pretty clear, with the absolute x-y pixel positioning of the images set with **LEFT** and **TOP** attributes. What may not be clear is the meaning of **Z-INDEX**. This allows you to specify the top-to-bottom priority of your layers: *The higher the value of Z-INDEX, the higher up the stack of layers a given layer will appear.* Here, the second layer stacks on top the first.

You might wonder why Netscape has engineered a separate, but virtually equal, means of layering Web pages, particularly since it supports the W³ draft standard. Well, even though you can position your elements with either method, the W³ standard doesn't allow for anything to be done with the objects once they're positioned. To make DHTML **dynamic**, something else is needed. Here is where Netscape and Microsoft diverge on DHTML.

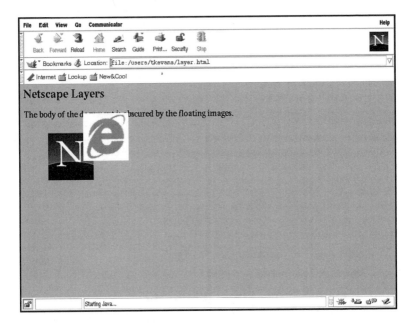

Figure 20.2   Netscape layers.

Netscape layers can be manipulated, after a page containing them has been loaded, by using JavaScript. Images may change or move around as the page loads, creating animations. In addition, an object may change as a result of a mouse event, such as moving the mouse over the object or clicking it. There's no room in this lesson, unfortunately, for an example of using JavaScript to manipulate Netscape layers; see **http://developer.netscape.com/ library/documentation/communicator/layers/** for more information.

NETSCAPE DOWNLOADABLE FONTS

One major complaint Web page designers have is the inability to absolutely control the fonts in which a document is rendered. Netscape DHTML allows style sheet markup to **attach** a specific set of fonts to a Web page which are downloaded with your HTML page.

> **No Free Lunches** You must own the right to use downloadable fonts, so be sure to observe all copyright limitations on any fonts you purchase or otherwise obtain. Note also, users who download your pages with attached fonts are prevented from saving and reusing them in other pages.

You'll recall from Lesson 16, "HTML Style Sheets in Action: Color in Your Web Pages," how you set up a style sheet rule for headlines:

H1 { color: green; font-size: 18pt; font-style: italic }

With Netscape DHTML, you can take this a step further and use a specific font:

H1 { color: green; font-size: 18pt; font-style: italic font-family: "Impress BT," }

Next, create a **font definition file**, using a tool like the Netscape Communicator **Font Composer** Plug-in. Finally, add a reference to your font definition file in your <STYLE> markup; here's the syntax:

<STYLE TYPE="text/css">

@fontdef url(http://www.mycompany.com/ myfonts/fonts.pfr");

</STYLE>

MICROSOFT'S DHTML

Microsoft also supports the W^3 draft on the positioning of HTML elements using style sheets, but has implemented two major differences in its version of DHTML. They are:

- A comprehensive **object model** for the HTML language, under which all elements can be treated as manipulatible objects

- **Data binding**, which allows the browser client to manipulate data downloaded from a Web server

To understand these concepts, you need to know Microsoft views DHTML in a much larger sense than Netscape. Specifically, under Microsoft's view, any aspect of documents you've already downloaded with your browser can and will change afterwards, with no further interaction with the Web server from which they came.

Earlier, you learned that JavaScript can allow changes in Web pages after they've been downloaded, and if this still seems no different than Netscape's model, you need to know one more subtle thing. JavaScript code in Web pages gets run only *once*, at the time the page is downloaded. While JavaScript authors can anticipate and provide for events, like mouse movements, and do some data verification in forms, the script never gets reread based on anything the user might do. Through the use of the comprehensive object model, Microsoft DHTML allows all aspects of a Web page to be subject to DHTML.

Figures 20.3 and 20.4 show an example page from Microsoft's DHTML gallery (**http://www.microsoft.com/gallery/files/ html/default.htm**). It's a table of stock share information, with headings for the stock's trading symbol, current price, price change, and volume. Clicking any of the table headings resorts and redisplays the table using the selected heading as the sort key.

Symbol	Quote	Change	Volume
AAPL	16.5625	0.01875	2057300
AOL	43.75	-0.25	1397600
BORL	8	0.125	267900
HWP	55.375	-0.25	2552200
IBM	143.625	0.75	2005800
MSFT	99	-0.625	7665900
NSCP	27	-0.375	1466100

FIGURE 20.3   Microsoft DHTML Repeated Table I.

This example uses DHTML data binding, with the data displayed in the standard HTML table being pulled from an external source. Besides ordinary HTML tables markup, this one uses the new DHTML table attributes **<DATASRC>** and **<DATAPAGESIZE>**. This means the table itself is drawn using regular HTML table markup, but the data is dynamically pulled from some other source, say, an Access database. Clicking one of the headings reaccesses the external data, resorts it, and then repopulates the table with the rearranged data. Figure 20.4 shows the table re-sorted on the Change column.

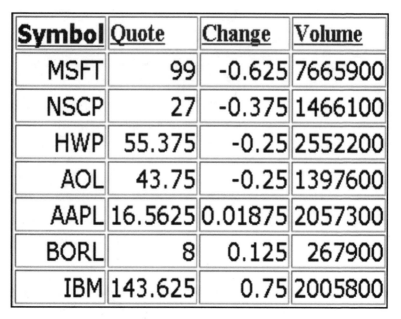

Symbol	Quote	Change	Volume
MSFT	99	-0.625	7665900
NSCP	27	-0.375	1466100
HWP	55.375	-0.25	2552200
AOL	43.75	-0.25	1397600
AAPL	16.5625	0.01875	2057300
BORL	8	0.125	267900
IBM	143.625	0.75	2005800

FIGURE 20.4   Microsoft DHTML Repeated Table II.

DHTML STANDARDS

You've already learned about the draft standard for positioning of HTML elements using style sheets, supported by both Microsoft and Netscape. It's a safe bet what we've called Generic DHTML will be included in the final HTML 4.0 standard.

What about the differences, then? It would seem Microsoft has a leg up, since there is also a draft W^3 standard on the Document Object Model (see **http://www.w3.org/MarkUp/DOM/**). However, since it was Microsoft itself which proposed this draft, you can be sure Netscape will have some say in its final disposition.

> **A Wink Is as Good as a Nod to a Blind Horse**
> Microsoft has recently adopted an unusual attitude toward the W^3 standards process. It announced it would no longer make unilateral, proprietary changes in HTML. Rather, any changes would be first *submitted* to the W^3. Of course, under this posture, Microsoft would then consider itself free to unilaterally introduce the changes, without waiting for W^3 *approval.*

At the same time, it would appear the advancement of purely proprietary HTML tags like <LAYER> runs counter to recent standards activities. Because Netscape is unlikely to give up on its own new tag, however, expect some sort of accommodation *à la* the <OBJECT> abstraction you learned in Lesson 17.

This lesson has introduced the hot new subject of Dynamic HTML, even though much of its activity is outside the HTML 4.0 standard, as if to prove how standards continue to evolve almost as fast as they are implemented. In the next lesson, you'll learn about tools for creating and editing HTML documents.

21 · _{L E S S O N}

HTML EDITORS

In this lesson, you learn about several HTML editors and other tools for creating HTML documents.

Although, as you've learned, you can create and edit HTML documents using a variety of tools you already have on your computer, you may want to consider the growing number of HTML-specific tools.

WHY DO I NEED AN EDITOR, THEN?

The primary reason people want HTML-specific editors is the desire to have **WYSIWYG (What You See Is What You Get)** capabilities. Naturally, you'd like to see your HTML documents rendered as you create them, with on-screen formatting. It's also convenient to have the ability to plop correct markup code right into a document by hitting a function key or using a pull-down menu instead of manually typing the code into the document. Best of all, you'd like to have the effects of your editing shown immediately on-screen. Finally, you probably have a lot of documents you'd like to convert easily into HTML.

We've saved the discussion of these editors until now because it's important for you to have a fundamental understanding of HTML and how it works. Getting your fingers dirty typing in HTML markup gives you a feel for the language and, more importantly, helps you visualize what's possible with a little imagination. HTML editors are great, but they don't give you this basic grounding in the language. With your basic grounding in HTML, you'll be able to fully appreciate and utilize the features of the tools described in this lesson.

Types of Editors/Editing Tools

There are three basic kinds of HTML editors/editing tools:

- **Tricks** and **add-ons** for your own word processor for editing HTML.
- Tools to **convert** existing documents to HTML.
- Full-blown, **WYSIWYG HTML editors**.

> **Fore?** It's likely the HTML editing tools described in this lesson may either not support the HTML 4.0 standard or may not yet be available in versions which do. Be sure to check the Web sites mentioned in this lesson for the latest versions.

Tricks, Add-ons, and Converters

You can use your familiar word processor to create HTML and get a leg up on the task with one or more of the following tricks, add-ons, and converters.

Word Processor Tricks and Add-Ons

If you've been using your word processor to create HTML documents, you already have the ability to create some tools to make HTML editing easier. You've probably already thought of them, but let's mention them anyway. All modern word processors have features for creating and reusing commonly used procedures. These are usually called **macros**. It's a very simple matter to create macros for each of the major HTML markup tags, and then save them for later. Each time you need to add an HTML markup code to your document, you can just grab your pull-down macro menu, or hit whatever function key your word processor uses, and zap in the markup you want.

Macros   Word processors allow you to record and save these as a series of keystrokes, then play them back to automate repetitive tasks.

You can also create (or obtain on the Internet) document **templates/style sheets** for HTML markup. Even simple word processor **global search-and-replace** features can help speed up creation of HTML documents.

RECENT WORD PROCESSORS SUPPORT HTML DIRECTLY

Microsoft Word version 7.0 and higher directly supports creating and editing HTML. In addition, you can convert existing Word documents into HTML with an enhanced **Save As** capability. Figure 21.1 shows Word 97 in HTML mode with its **Insert, Forms** pull-down activated. As you can see from the screenshot, Word allows point-and-click insertion of Forms and other markup. Word's archrival, Corel WordPerfect, has the same capabilities in versions 7 and higher, but goes a step further in supporting full-blown SGML, the standard generalized markup language, of which HTML is a subset.

If you're not running the latest, greatest version of either Word or WordPerfect, you can get free add-ons to some older versions to support HTML. WordPerfect 6 users can download Corel's *Internet Publisher* at **ftp://ftp.corel.com/pub/WordPerfect**, while Microsoft *Internet Assistant* is available at **http:// www.microsoft.com/msword/internet/ia**. Both companies have also made available, at no cost, stand-alone viewers for their documents, Microsoft *Word Viewer* and Corel *Envoy* can be used as Helper applications with Web browsers. These read-only viewers allow you to put standard (that is, not-converted-to-HTML) word processing documents on your Web site; users with the viewers can access them, in much the same way Adobe Portable Document Format (pdf) documents can be viewed with *Acrobat Reader*.

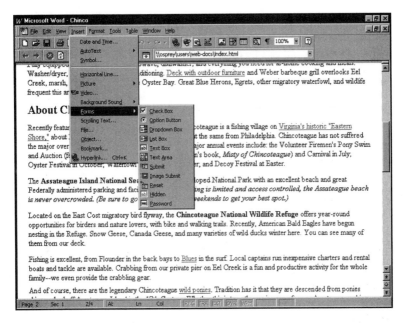

FIGURE 21.1   Microsoft Word 97 in HTML mode.

> **TIP**
>
> **Also Offered**   Microsoft and Corel also have added HTML capabilities to other programs in their product "suites," such as PowerPoint/Corel Presentations, Excel/Quattro, Access, and Corel Central. You can also find HTML add-ons and/or read-only viewers for earlier versions of some of these products at the companies' Web sites.

DOCUMENT CONVERTERS

You no doubt already have documents you'd like to have available on your Web server. You've already learned about recent versions of major word processors and their ability to convert common word processor documents to HTML. Even if you're using very old word processors, you may still be able to convert your documents in a simple, two-step process.

First, most word processors have a **Save As** feature that saves documents in alternative formats. One common such format is called the **Rich Text Format**, or **RTF**. RTF makes documents portable, while preserving document formatting.

Although RTF was developed by Microsoft, it's widely supported and converting from RTF to most any other format is fairly simple. You may have used it to convert from one word processor format to another, such as from Word to WordPerfect. A shareware software package called **RTFtoHTML** (for UNIX systems, PCs, and Macs) is available to, as the name suggests, convert RTF documents to HTML. You'll find the conversion less than perfect, especially if you have complex tabular material or graphics in the original documents. Nevertheless, the main job of converting the documents to HTML is done well. You'll find these packages on the Web at **http://www.sunpack.com/RTF/latest/**.

The main advantage of the two-stage RTF conversion process is that you can convert your existing documents to HTML quickly and easily. The disadvantage, as with word processor macros, is you're still not working in a WYSIWYG environment. In addition, you should expect to have to do some cleanup editing of the resulting HTML documents.

Besides this two-step **RTFtoHTML conversion method**, there are several other document converters. Of particular interest are those that convert from *FrameMaker*, a widely used desktop publishing package, to HTML. These include a commercial package called *WebWorks Publisher* from Quadralay and several freeware packages, *Frame2htmL* and *WEBMAKER*. Release 5 (and higher) of *FrameMaker* have built-in HTML support. Also, Interleaf, Inc.'s *Cyberleaf* converts not only among different word processor formats, but also from any of them to HTML. Adobe's *PageMaker* product also does a wide variety of document conversion, including to and from HTML.

Finally, there are a wide variety of other programs that convert from one text format or another to HTML, including those that convert from:

- The TeX and LaTeX formatting languages widely used by scientists and mathematicians
- UNIX **nroff/troff** and **man** pages
- Other less well-known formats

Full-Blown HTML Editors

If you're ready to move on from your text editor or word processor, you may want to look at one of several full-blown HTML editors. These operate in a more or less WYSIWYG environment, rendering your document formatting pretty much as it will look in a Web browser. This is a crowded market, so let's take quick looks at just a few of the major editors.

SoftQuad HoTMetaL

SoftQuad *HoTMetaL* is available in both a no-cost version (**http://www.sq.com/**) and a commercial version, the latter of which is called *HoTMetaL PRO*. At the time this book was being written, HoTMetaL PRO version 4 was available for Windows 95/NT only, though other platforms may be supported by the time you read this. *HoTMetaL* version 3.0 was available as freeware. Again, this may have changed by now. The latest version of the package contains a number of tools, including a personal Web server, a guided Web Site Maker, Cascading Style Sheet editor, image-map support, Frames editor, foreign document converter, database-enabling software, Java and VRML (Virtual Reality Markup Language) editors, and an animated GIF image tool.

Sausage Software's Hot Dog

One of the most popular commercial HTML editors for Windows PCs is called *Hot Dog*, from the Australian firm Sausage Software. Like *HoTMetaL*, *Hot Dog* uses pull-down menus and an extensive toolbar to make creation of HTML documents easier. Of particular note, *Hot Dog* version 4.0 has:

- A drag-and-drop **Resource Manager** for inserting links, graphics, and other documents

- A **text color picker**, which allows you to preview your text and background colors

- An **automated downloader**, which will update your copy of *Hot Dog* as new features are added or bugs fixed

Calling itself the "Switzerland of the Web," Sausage Software has taken a position of neutrality in the HTML standards wars. All features of the HTML 4.0 standard are supported, along with all of the Netscape and Microsoft extensions. To help you negotiate the several standards, *Hot Dog* allows you to switch on and off support for specific HTML rulesets, such as Microsoft-specific markup. Figure 21.2 shows Hot Dog. You can check out *HotDog* at **http:// www.sausage.com/**.

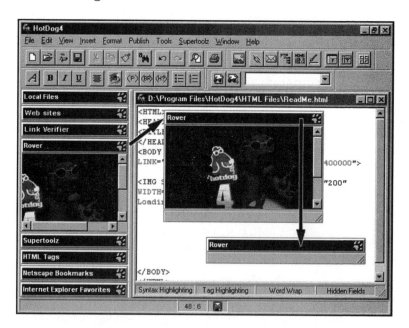

FIGURE 21.2 Hot Dog 4.0.

NETSCAPE COMPOSER

The Netscape Communicator package includes an integrated browser/editor product called *Composer;* the entire package is

available at **http://home.netscape.com/**. *Composer* shares
many of the features of the other editors described. What distinguishes *Composer* is its true WYSIWYG capability, including display of in-line images, as shown in Figure 21.3. The entire
Netscape Communicator package, including *Composer*, is available
for PCs, the Mac, and for several UNIX systems, although Composer isn't compliant with the HTML 4 standard.

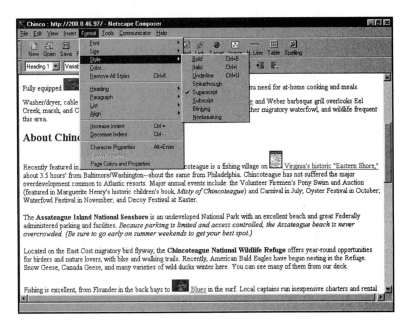

FIGURE 21.3   Netscape Composer.

MICROSOFT FRONTPAGE/FRONTPAD

Microsoft seems to be sending off mixed signals with respect to an
HTML editor. As you've already seen, Word itself has extensive
HTML capabilities. In addition, Microsoft sells a high-end package
called *FrontPage*, which is much like Netscape *Composer* in its
capabilities (*FrontPage 98* was in beta test at the time this book
went to press). Perhaps as a response to *Composer*'s full integration
into the Netscape Communicator package, *Internet Explorer*

version 4 now includes *FrontPage Express*, a stripped-down version of *FrontPage*.

ADOBE PAGEMILL FOR MACINTOSH AND WINDOWS 95

PageMill is far and away the favorite Macintosh HTML editor. Version 2.0 of this package is available for Windows 95 and the Macintosh. *PageMill* has support for many of the latest HTML enhancements, including frames, tables, and animated images.

Also, the package supports WYSIWYG editing, including internal support for Netscape-style plug-ins, allowing dynamic viewing (what you hear is what you get?) of multimedia files right in the editor. With Macintosh-style drag-and-drop support, *PageMill* features HTML frames and table editors, a built-in spelling checker and integrated image support, support for Java, and corporate database connectivity. Client-side image maps are supported as well.

On the minus side, *PageMill* doesn't have all the integrated "Web publishing" features other HTML editors, including Netscape *Composer*, Microsoft *FrontPage*, and others have. These other packages allow the direct upload of documents to Web servers right out of the HTML editor via pull-down menus. With *PageMill*, you'll need to pop into the included Web site manager, *SiteMill*, to place your Web pages. For more information about PageMill, see Adobe's Web site, **http://www.adobe.com/**.

OTHER HTML EDITING TOOLS

Besides these shareware and commercial HTML tools and editors, there are dozens of others, both free and commercial. Check out the World Wide Web Consortium's *Tools for WWW Providers* page at **http://www.w3.org/pub/WWW/Tools**.

This lesson has covered quite a lot of ground concerning HTML editors. We've discussed the pros and cons of using plain-text editors, word-processor tricks and add-ons, document converters, and full-blown WYSIWYG HTML editors. In the next lesson, you learn about preformatted text and HTML mathematics.

Preformatted Text and HTML Math in Your HTML Documents

In this lesson, the first of two catch-all lessons on other aspects of HTML, you learn how to use HTML markup to format tabular material without using HTML table markup. In addition, you'll be introduced to future HTML standards (and current workarounds) for displaying mathematical expressions on Web pages.

You learned in Lesson 10, "Creating Tables," to use HTML table markup to create tabular material and to fine-tune the layout of your Web pages using table markup. We're returning to this subject because you need to be aware some older Web browsers, however, don't support tables, or they do so only partially, or display them slightly differently. Still others (NCSA X Mosaic for UNIX) allow users to turn table support on and off, while another (NCSA WinMosaic) allows users to set table display preferences that may cause your tables to be displayed differently than you intended. If users who will be viewing your Web pages use older Web browsers, you'll need to consider another way of preserving essential layout, such as tables in your HTML documents.

Including Preformatted Text

Short of using HTML table markup, the sure way to retain the formatting of your tables is to use **preformatted text**. If viewers of your HTML documents don't have table-capable browsers—

such as the Lynx nongraphical browser—or browsers with limited/configurable table support—such as NCSA Mosaic—you'll want to know how to set up preformatted text.

Generally speaking, HTML ignores the extra white space you'd normally use in a table to create rows and columns; the **<PRE>** HTML tag **preserves** it. This is where tabular material comes in, since tables have specific spacing/white space needs in order to create and line up the rows and columns. Here's a simple fragment of HTML using the **<PRE>** tag to create a small table, much like the one you created in the last lesson:

<PRE>Row 1   Column 1   Column 2

Row 2   Column 1   Column 2</PRE>

As you can see, this is a simple two-row, two-column listing. Without the preformatting tags, this text would run together on a single line in your Web browser, with no extra white space, like this:

Row 1 Column 1 Column 2 Row 2 Column 1 Column 2

The **<PRE>** tag causes this text to be rendered in the tabular format you want.

> **Dress 'Em Up**   When working with preformatted text, it's not a good idea to use tabs to create white space. Web browsers differ in the way they interpret the Tab character, so you should use individual **spaces** to make sure columns of material line up. In the preceding example, we used exactly five spaces between the columns. Unfortunately, this can get tedious.

The **<PRE>** tag has one optional **attribute** you can include. You can specify the **width** of your preformatted text like this:

<PRE WIDTH="65">This formatted text is limited to 65 characters wide</PRE>

Let's re-create the Consolidated HTML Consultants table from Lesson 10 using preformatted text:

<HTML><HEAD><TITLE>Consolidated HTML Consultants</TITLE></HEAD><BODY>

<H1>Consolidated HTML Consultants, Inc.</H1>

<H2>1994 Profit and Loss (Actual and Forecast) </H2>

<PRE WIDTH="60">

First Quarter   Second Quarter   Third Quarter Fourth Quarter

---

12% Profit (Actual)   2% Loss (Actual)   5% Loss (Actual)   8% Profit (Actual)

11% profit (Forecast) 2% profit(Forecast) 3% loss (Forecast) 5% profit (Forecast)</PRE><BODY></ HTML>

Here, we used standard HTML headline markup (two different levels) to add **headings** for our quarterly report, and used preformatted text to add column headings, a horizontal ruler (consisting of a simple row of hyphens), and the two rows of **data**. Figure 22.1 shows our table. As you can see, you can come pretty close to the table formatting you learned in Lesson 10 with some imaginative use of HTML.

> **TIP** **Converting Existing Documents with Tables** In Lesson 21, "HTML Editors," you learned about a package called *rtftohtml*, which allows you to convert existing documents that have been saved in the Microsoft Rich Text Format into HTML. Where such documents have tabular material in them, it'll be converted to preformatted text to preserve the spacing.

```
File   Edit   View   Go   Communicator                                        Help
 ◄     ►     ▲     ⌂     ⚲     ⬡     ⬛     ⬜     ⬚                        N
Back  Forward Reload  Home  Search  Guide  Print...  Security  Stop

 Bookmarks    Location: file:/users/tkevans/wabi/winword6/tmg2html/pre-tab.htm
 Internet   Lookup   New&Cool

Consolidated HTML Consultants, Inc.

1994 Profit and Loss (Actual and Forecast)

First Quarter          Second Quarter       Third Quarter       Fourth Quarter
----------------------------------------------------------------------------
12% Profit (Actual)    2% Loss (Actual)     5% Loss (Actual)    8% Profit (Actual)
11% profit (Forecast)  2% profit(Forecast)  3% loss (Forecast)  5% profit (Forecast)




 100%
```

FIGURE 22.1   Table created using preformatted text.

MATHEMATICAL EXPRESSIONS IN HTML

As with the HTML 3.2 standard, support for mathematical markup in HTML 4.0 has not been included. The W3's work in this area continues, and may have come to fruition when the final HTML 4.0 specification is published.

Conventional formatting of math expressions on the printed page relies on sophisticated typesetting capabilities still not available in HTML. The main problem with mathematical expressions is the use of multiple **ascenders** and **descenders**. While HTML supports simple subscripts (**<SUB>**) and superscripts (**<SUP>**), support for the complex, multiple levels of ascenders and descenders needed isn't available. Other problems include use of special symbols and the fact that even common symbols, such as parentheses, change size depending on the expressions.

Since HTML sprang up in the scientific community, the need to include mathematical notation in Web pages has been long recognized, and several workarounds have been developed. Most of these workarounds, such as the **LaTeX2HTML** package developed by Niko Drakos (**http://cbl.leeds.ac.uk/nikos/ tex2html/doc/latex2html/latex2html.html**), involve the conversion of mathematical expressions into *inline images* for inclusion on Web pages.

LaTEX2HTML and other similar approaches are based on the **TeX** family of computer typesetting languages, widely used in the scientific and mathematical community. Written in *Perl* (often used for CGI-bin scripts; see Lesson 14, "Fill-In Forms and CGI Scripts"), LaTeX2HTML converts math expressions into small GIF images and generates HTML documents containing them.

Imaged-based math expressions in Web pages are useful, but not satisfactory, for a couple of reasons. The main reason is the quality of the images, but the inability to index and or search on the content of the image/expressions is also a problem. Finally, as you learned in Lesson 11, "Adding Images to Your Document," images add to the bandwidth requirements of Web pages, and users who suppress the display of images won't see them.

Disappearing Differential Equations   Another major problem with image-based math in HTML pages lies in text and background colors. Users who set up their Web browsers to use colors they prefer may not be able to view images containing math expressions if the color sets conflict.

As a result of these limitations, other approaches have arisen. IBM's **techexplorer** plug-in (**http://www.ics.raleigh.ibm.com/ ics/techexp.htm**), for instance, reads TeX-formatted documents directly and renders them on the spot in your browser window (see Figure 22.2). Other approaches include the use of Java applets to render math expressions.

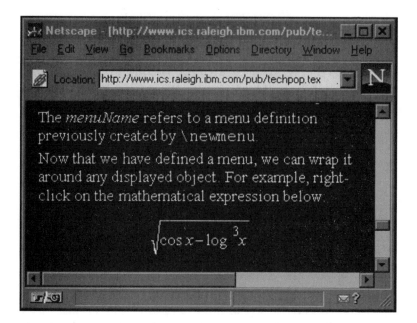

FIGURE 22.2   IBM TechExplorer plug-in renders math expressions.

The W3's HTML Math working group continues its efforts to develop true HTML markup that can be rendered by Web browsers directly, rather than requiring conversions, images, or plug-ins. To this end, current Mathematics Markup Language (**MathML**) drafts take the approach of defining math **objects** in an HTML page, which can contain the multi-level formatting needed for ascenders and descenders. MathML includes two main kinds of elements, those containing numbers and symbols, and (usually nested) elements, containing both formatting and data tags. In addition, MathML uses an **<EXPR>** element, which can contain **content** tags that unambiguously encode the meaning of expressions.

You can check into the current status of MathML at **http://www.w3.org/MarkUp/Math/**.

This lesson focused on preformatted text and emerging math markup. In the next lesson, you'll pick up a number of HTML subjects that don't quite fit in any other lesson.

OTHER ASPECTS OF HTML 4.0

In this lesson, you'll learn several miscellaneous aspects of HTML 4.0, including support for different international languages, use of about-this-document markup, and WebCasting and channels.

INTERNATIONAL LANGUAGE SUPPORT IN HTML 4.0

So far in this book, all you've learned about HTML 4.0 is pretty much language independent. For the most part, document formatting and other HTML markup is language-neutral; an image, hyperlink, or URL is the same in any language. However, there is a need for support of languages other than English in HTML, and HTML 4.0 provides a generic means of it.

The *printed appearance* of languages differs in any of a number of ways, however, including:

- The character set used (Western languages versus Eastern languages)

- Directional flow of the printed page (left to right or right to left)

- Other minor differences, such as diacritical marks, special characters, hyphenation, and so on

HTML 4.0 allows you to select specific international languages for your Web pages. In addition, you can mix languages within individual pages, and control the directional flow of pages.

SPECIFYING AN OVERALL LANGUAGE FOR AN HTML DOCUMENT

Designating a particular overall language for your HTML documents is a simple matter. To do so, use the **LANG** attribute at the beginning of your document. Here's the simplest example:

<HTML LANG="en-US">

...rest of your HTML document

</HTML>

As you can see, your language selection is nearly the first thing in the document, just after the declaration that the document is in HTML.

You might recognize the **en-US** value for the LANG attribute as the official International Standards Organization ISO-639 designation for U.S. English. HTML 4.0 accepts all the **ISO-639 language designations**.

 No, Not "In Search Of"   Where different versions of a language exist, such as U.S. and British English, you can use the specific ISO-639 code (*en-US* or *en-BR*). Otherwise, you can use a shorter, generic code; examples include *fr* (French), *it* (Italian), and *zh* (Chinese).

MIXING LANGUAGES IN HTML DOCUMENTS

You may need to include more than one language in your Web pages, and you can use the LANG attribute to do so. Use of this attribute is not limited to the top of your documents, as in the preceding example. LANG can appear pretty much anywhere in your HTML, provided it makes sense. Suppose you want a paragraph of German to appear in the middle of your otherwise English document:

```
<HTML LANG="en-US">
...text of English part...
<P LANG="DE">Paragraph in German</P>
...English text resumes
</HTML>
```

You can even mix in individual words or phrases from another language in your document, using LANG as an attribute to, say, <EM> (emphasized text), like this:

The motto of the French Revolution of 1789 was

<EM LANG="FR">Liberte, Egalite, Fraternite</EM>

DIRECTION OF TEXT FLOW

Of course, some languages—Hebrew, Arabic, and others—have a fundamental difference: They flow from right to left on the printed page. HTML 4.0 allows you to specify the direction of text flow in your documents, using the **DIR** attribute.

 Not a Directory Listing   Don't confuse the DIR attribute with the deprecated attribute of the same name for directory lists. (See Lesson 9, "Creating Lists.")

As with the LANG attribute itself, you can specify the overall text flow in a document:

<HTML LANG="HE" DIR="RTL">

Document appears in Hebrew, right to left

</HTML>

You can also mix text-flow directions in your documents, just as you did with languages. Let's add some, say, Spanish to the previous example:

<HTML LANG="HE" DIR="RTL">

Document appears in Hebrew, right to left

<P LANG="ES" DIR="LTR">Paragraph in Spanish, left to right</P>

Document resumes in Hebrew, right to left

</HTML>

META-INFORMATION IN HTML

HTML 3.2 provides a means for you to include **about-this-document** information in your Web pages. While such **meta-information** doesn't actually show in your documents when people view them, it can be useful in a number of ways, since Web browsers read and process the information as they load the pages.

Use the **<META>** element within the **<HEAD>** portion of your HTML pages to include information about the document, such as its author, expiration date, and key words for search engine use (see Lesson 24, "Announcing Your Web Pages to the World").

If you have a page that changes frequently, such as a *What's New* page, you can specify a short expiration date as meta-information to ensure your readers always get the current version when they visit it, rather than an older copy that may be in their browser's disk cache. Here's an example:

<HTML><HEAD <META http-equiv="Expires" contents="Sun,

27 July 1998 00:00:00 GMT">

Web browsers accessing this page analyze this information (it says the document expires on July 27, 1998, at midnight, Greenwich Mean Time). If that date has passed, the Web browser will attempt to retrieve the current version of the page, even if it has a recent copy in its cache.

> **Hand Over the Cache**   Replace the values for *http-equiv*
> and *contents* above with **Pragma** and **no-cache**, respec-
> tively, to prevent a document from being cached at all.
> Each time it's accessed, the very latest version will be
> loaded.
>
> TIP

As this book was being written, the HTML 4.0 draft standard was
incomplete with respect to meta-information. Proposals being
discussed included full bibliographic information, support for the
Platform for Internet Content Selection (PICS, designed to help
parents and teachers control what children can access on the
Web) initiative, code signing/authentication, privacy, and intel-
lectual property rights management. You'll want to check the
final HTML 4.0 standard for more information in this area. Of
particular note is the recent support by U.S. President Bill Clinton
for the PICS initiative.

WEBCASTING AND CHANNELS

The phenomenal success of PointCast (**http://
www.pointcast.com/**), with its user-customizable background
news- and information-retrieval capabilities, has led the development of what's called **push**. PointCast allows you to select one or
more specialized **channels** of information—stock prices or sports
news, say—that are automatically pushed to your system and
displayed in the PointCast screensaver. Once you've selected your
channels, the information is sent to your computer automatically,
without your having to ask for it; new information on your channels arrives automatically as well.

While many corporate network managers rightfully bemoan the
network bandwidth consumed by large numbers of employees
running PointCast on their idle PCs, the notion of *specialized
channels of information, pushed to users automatically,* has spread
rapidly, especially in corporate intranets. The ability to broadcast

corporate or organizational information to users' desktops automatically has spawned a number of commercial WebCasting initiatives.

Building an Intranet   For more information on corporate intranets, see the author's *Building an Intranet*, a hands-on guide to setting up an internal Web, published by Que's sister imprint Sams, ISBN 1-57521-071-1. You can view information about this and other books published by Macmillan Computer Publishing at the Macmillan SuperLibrary, **http://www.mcp.com/**.

HTML 4.0 does not mention WebCasting or push technology at all. Both Netscape and Microsoft have implemented push technology, but, unfortunately, the two methods are incompatible. Microsoft has submitted its **Channel Definition Format** (CDF) to the W³ Consortium—and gone ahead and implemented it in Internet Explorer version 4. Netscape claims everything that can be accomplished with CDF can be done with existing HTML-related technology, such as JavaScript and Java, and that a formal CDF is not needed. Both companies are furiously signing up commercial Channel Partners for the development of specialized Internet and intranet WebCasting.

A Pox on Both Your Houses   This situation shows the continuing Microsoft-Netscape bickering over HTML at its worst. Netscape sniffs and says nothing other than the technology it has already developed is necessary to implement push, as if its JavaScript, for instance, were really an "Open" technology. Microsoft takes a holier-than-thou stance, promising never to implement new things in HTML without first *proposing* them to the W³ Consortium, with no mention, of course, of whether the Consortium will ever *adopt* the proposals. Meanwhile, you, the HTML author, are left in the lurch trying to select a technology to use.

Microsoft's **Active Channel Content** uses a whole new set of HTML markup. Channel pages are HTML documents which can call sub-pages, **channel items** (also written in HTML). CDF markup specifies not only channel items, but also specifications for repeating intervals, expiration, and administrative aspects, such as logging. One particularly interesting feature of CDF is the ability to automatically distribute software updates on a corporate intranet. Users simply browse available channels with IE 4 and select those to which they want to subscribe. Channel icons are added to the new Active Desktop or the Windows QuickLaunch toolbar. For details on CDF, visit **http://www.microsoft.com/ workshop/prog/ie4/channels/cdf1-f.htm**.

Netscape's push technology is called NetCaster, and is built into Netscape Communicator. It uses **WebTops**, anchored to your PC desktop, which are linked to the channels you have selected with the NetCaster **Channel Finder**. HTML authors need no special HTML markup to create NetCaster channels. Simple channels can be created using an **Add Channel Wizard**, which will generate HTML and JavaScript based on information entered into a fill-in form. You'll need JavaScript programming skills for complex channels. To learn more about NetCaster Channels, visit **http:// developer.netscape.com/library/examples/**.

In this lesson, you've learned about support for international languages, HTML meta-information, and WebCasting and channels. The next lesson, the last in this *10 Minute Guide*, tells you how you can announce your Web pages to the world.

Announcing Your Web Pages to the World

24

In this lesson, you learn how to make your Web pages known to the outside world.

Once your HTML documents are up and running on a Web server, you'll want the world to know about them. Fortunately, there are a large number of forums for this kind of announcement. Most of them are Web **Search Engines**, searchable indexes of Web resources. Let's look at Search Engines, then at some other means of announcing your Web pages.

Search Engines and Your Web Pages

A large number of searchable indexes have grown up on the Web. While each is different, and get their information from a different mix of sources, Search Engines have much in common. Generally, users have the ability to type in one or more **search strings** (in some cases, you can enter natural language concepts) and have the Search Engine look for your specifications in its database. Netscape version 4 users know about the **Internet** button, usually displayed near the top of the standard Netscape browser window, which accesses the **Netscape Guide** that provides access to a number of Search Engines. Similarly, Internet Explorer 4's **exploring** button opens a page containing search engines. Figure 24.1 shows part of the results for a search on the word "cigars" in **eXcite (http://www.excite.com/)**; note how the Search Engine has suggested additional search words.

Natural Language Concepts Some search engines accept queries in ordinary sentences. For example, instead of asking for the search words "cigars" and "cuban," you might be able to say "Tell me about Cuban cigars."

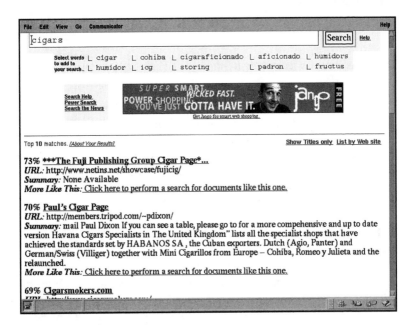

FIGURE 24.1   eXcite Search Engine results.

ADDING YOUR WEB PAGES TO SEARCH ENGINES

While each Search Engine seeks to be unique in some way, all allow users to add URLs to them, usually through a fill-in form. Most don't charge for such listings, though there are some which do. Either is a grand way of publicizing your own Web pages.

In Search Of   Of course, you can use the Search Engines themselves to look for announcement services; see, for example **http://www.yahoo.com/ Computers_and_Internet/World_Wide_Web/ Announcement_Services/**.

The Yahoo! Search Engine (**http://www.yahoo.com/**) has an add-an-URL form, which asks you to categorize your Web page, and also requests comments. What you enter helps build up Yahoo!'s keyword database, so be sure to use good descriptions of your pages. Other services don't require you to enter this information. Instead, they send out a **spider** (sometimes called a **robot**, or **'bot**) to access and search the URL you've entered to add to their database. Spiders typically will follow all links in the URL you've specified, so all your Web pages will get indexed as well. Later in this lesson, you'll learn how to bait your Web pages for 'bots, to ensure they're indexed the way you want them to be.

Before we move on, you need to know a few more things about Yahoo!. First, if you use the service, you'll see it's indexed down to what seems infinite detail. The Web is populated by a vocal minority of people who actually like this sort of endless indexing, so you may want to take the time to wander around in Yahoo! until you find just the right place for your service. Every Yahoo! page has the Add hyperlink on it, and when you click it from a place in the index hierarchy, the category on the fill-in form will be filled in for you.

You might even want to install your own Search Engine if you're running a corporate intranet, to index multiple Web sites within your company. eXcite's Search Engine software, **EWS** (eXcite for Web Servers), is available for free download at **http://www.excite.com/navigate/**. EWS is available for Windows NT and UNIX servers, but is an unsupported product.

> **TIP** **Search Engine Leveraging: Submit-It** This is a good example of a no-charge service through which you can add your Web page URLs to multiple Search Engines at the same time; see **http://www.submit-it.com/**. **AAA Internet Promotions** is a commercial service that will add your URL to many Search Engines' databases. You can visit AAA Internet Promotions at **http://www.websitepromote.com/**. Some of these allow literally anything to be posted, from business listings to adult entertainment to radical politics. As a result, you may find yourself with some pretty strange bedfellows if you put information about your Web resources on some of these.

WHAT'S NEW PAGES

What's New pages are a Web tradition. Many Web sites use them for announcements of new pages and services; you'll probably want to set one up for your own Web site or intranet. The great ancestor of all What's New pages (NCSA What's New) is no longer maintained, though you can look through its archives at **http://www.ncsa.uiuc.edu/SDG/Software/Mosaic/Docs/whats-new.html**.

> **TIP** **Evergreen** What's New pages are important traffic builders for a Web site, particularly for a corporate intranet, provided you keep them up-to-date. If you want to use a What's New page of your own, be sure there's something new on it every day if possible. Train users to come to your What's New page by giving them new information frequently.

You've probably also noticed the **New & Cool** navigational button in Netscape version 4. Unfortunately, where Netscape used to allow submissions to its What's New page, this no longer seems to be the case. What gets chosen for the page, like who gets into *Planet Hollywood*, is anybody's guess: The page's maintainers know what they want, and recognize it when they see it.

Yahoo!, the Search Engine described earlier in this lesson, has a What's New page at **http://www.yahoo.com/new/**. There, you'll find a week's worth of daily listings of new pages; each daily entry lists as many as 2,000 new listings, so it would appear anything new that's added shows up here. Figure 24.2 shows the Yahoo! What's New page.

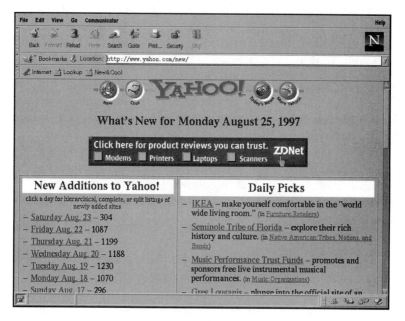

FIGURE 24.2   Yahoo! What's New Page.

LETTING 'BOTS DO THE WORK

Earlier, you learned some Search Engine Add-URL pages allow you to enter keywords describing your pages. Search engine Spiders/ Robots will search and index publicly accessible Web pages, but you can force feed them the keywords you choose in order to get better indexing. (Otherwise, 'bots treat every word in a document exactly alike.) In Lesson 23, "Other Aspects of HTML 4.0," you learned about using the **<META>** HTML tag to bundle about-this-document information inside the <HEAD> section of a Web page. There, you used <META> to:

- Include an expiration date for a document
- Suppress caching of a document

Meta-information about a Web page can also include a list of keywords of your choice about the document. Suppose, for example, you have a seaside resort rental property you advertise on the Web. To prime Web 'bots, add keywords like this:

> **<META NAME="KEYWORDS" LANG="en-US"**
> **CONTENT="beach resort rental condo vacation sea-**
> **side birdwatching nature fishing swimming luxury**
> **seaside sunbathing">**

You can include as many keywords as you'd like. Be sure to include synonyms as the example shows; you never know what words people will type into Search Engine forms. Visiting robots will pick up your keywords and give them more weight in indexing your pages than the rest of the page.

As the example shows, you can specify the language of your document to enhance indexing. If your Web site is truly international, you'll be maintaining different versions of your pages in several languages. While you will want to specify keywords in each document, you can have search engines treat your documents as a group for indexing purposes using the **<LINK>** tag. Here's an example associating three versions of the same document:

> **<HEAD><LINK LANG="es" TITLE="Spanish Version"**
> **REL="alternate" href="http://**
> **www.mycompany.com/spanish.html">**
>
> **<LINK LANG="fr" TITLE="French Version"**
> **REL="alternate" href="http://**
> **www.mycompany.com/french.html">**

<LINK LANG="en-US" TITLE="English Version" REL="alternate" href="http://www.mycompany.com/english.html"></HEAD>

Here, using the <LINK> tag and its attribute REL, we've associated the three documents. Just place your keywords using the <META> tag in each document. Search engines will pick up the links among the documents and index them together, rather than as unrelated documents.

Keep Out!   While this lesson has been about announcing your Web pages, you may want to keep some part of your Web site off limits to search engine 'bots. You can post no-trespassing signs on part of your Web site, by creating a plain text file called **robots.txt**. Here's an example of a robots.txt file, denying access to a branch of a Web site that has the top-level directory (or folder) name *private*.

User-agent: *

Disallow: /private

With this file in place, all directories of the Web site *except* the one named *private* will be indexed. For more information on the robots.txt file, see **http://infocrawler.com/mak/projects/robots/exclusion.html**.

Usenet Newsgroups

You'll want to announce your HTML resources on the mother of all computer bulletin boards, Usenet (also called NetNews). If you have access to NetNews, post a message about your resource to the newsgroup **comp.infosystems.www.announce**. This newsgroup is **moderated**, which means your announcement won't go out onto Usenet right away. Instead it'll be e-mailed to the newsgroup moderator, who will review it to make sure it conforms with the newsgroup's charter, and then post it. The

comp.infosystems.www.announce newsgroup's **charter**, describing its purpose and the procedures for posting to it, is posted to the group periodically. Also, look for the FAQs (Frequently Asked Questions) that are posted on a regular basis; one important such posting is titled "FAQ: How to Announce Your New Web Site," available on the Web at **http://ep.com/faq/ webannounce.html**.

You can also post an announcement of your Web resource to the newsgroup **comp.internet.net-happenings**, which is an unmoderated newsgroup. Whatever you post there appears without any review or editing.

OTHER MEANS OF ANNOUNCING YOUR WEB RESOURCES

If you're planning on doing business on the World Wide Web, don't overlook your normal advertising channels. If, for example, you advertise your services in computer-related publications, be sure to include the URL for your company's home page in your advertisements. Pick up any computer publication and you'll see most ads have URLs in them. You may even want to include your URL in mainstream advertisements, regardless of media. All the U.S. television news organizations, especially the television networks, heavily promote their Web sites in on-air advertisements, for example. In fact, a significant and gsóing portion of television commercials and print media advertisement seem to include URLs, and, more and more, you're hearing radio commercials intoning URLs.

If you're a regular Internet e-mail or NetNews user, you already know people frequently include **signature tags** on their e-mail messages and NetNews postings. Consider adding the URL to your Web server in your own signature tag. Some Web Search Engines scan every Usenet posting, looking for URLs, which then get added to the searchable databases; just by having your URL in your signature file, yours gets added every time you post. This is much like an online business card; every time you send e-mail or post NetNews, you'll be promoting your Web resources. Speaking of business cards, don't forget to put your URL on your printed one.

Sign It! It's common for Internet users to attach a small signature to all their e-mail messages and NetNews postings. This may give their postal address, phone number, or other similar information. In addition, many people use it for personal expression, including a favorite quotation, piece of song lyric, or other material they believe to be cute, funny, or otherwise significant. Many of these are tedious, juvenile, and significant only to the poster. Remember, they get attached *automatically* to every e-mail message you send, so make sure you really, really want yours to be seen again and again, by your boss, your co-workers, your significant other, and your children. Also, please, keep yours short: there's nothing like one-line e-mail messages with 25 lines of drivel attached as a signature.

In this final lesson of this *10 Minute Guide*, you've learned about publicizing your Web resources on the Internet.

Readers interested in extending their Web sites into corporate intranets may want to check out the author's best-selling book *Building an Intranet*, also published by Macmillan Computer Publishing, ISBN 1-57521-071-1. You can preview *Building an Intranet*, and other Macmillan books, at the Macmillan Information SuperLibrary on the Web at **http://www.mcp.com/**. Also, you can find more information about the author, and his other Web-related books, at **http://www.tkevans.com/tkevans.html**.

INDEX

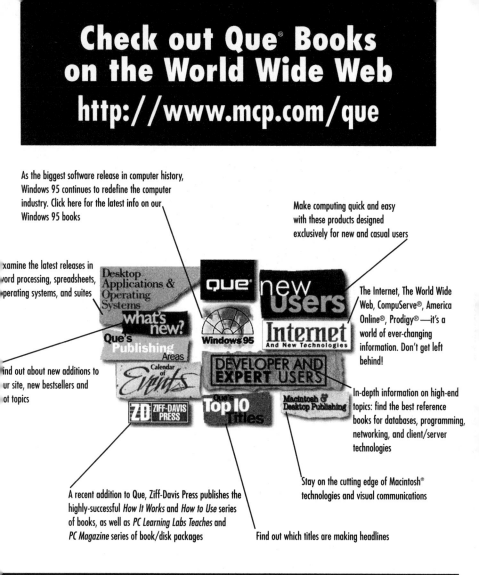

MACMILLAN COMPUTER PUBLISHING USA
A V I A C O M C O M P A N Y

Technical ----┐
            └--- **Support:**

If you need assistance with the information in this book or with a CD/Disk
accompanying the book, please access the Knowledge Base on our Web
site at **http://www.superlibrary.com/general/support**. Our most
Frequently Asked Questions are answered there. If you do not find the
answer to your questions on our Web site, you may contact Macmillan
Technical Support **(317) 581-3833** or e-mail us at **support@mcp.com**.

Complete and Return this Card
for a *FREE* Computer Book Catalog

Thank you for purchasing this book! You have purchased a superior computer book written expressly for your needs. To continue to provide the kind of up-to-date, pertinent coverage you've come to expect from us, we need to hear from you. Please take a minute to complete and return this self-addressed, postage-paid form. In return, we'll send you a free catalog of all our computer books on topics ranging from word processing to programming and the internet.

Mr. ☐   Mrs. ☐   Ms. ☐   Dr. ☐

Name (first) ☐☐☐☐☐☐☐☐☐☐   (M.I.) ☐   (last) ☐☐☐☐☐☐☐☐☐☐☐☐

Address ☐☐☐☐☐☐☐☐☐☐☐☐☐☐☐☐☐☐☐☐☐☐☐

☐☐☐☐☐☐☐☐☐☐☐☐☐☐☐☐☐☐☐☐☐☐☐

City ☐☐☐☐☐☐☐☐☐☐☐☐☐   State ☐☐   Zip ☐☐☐☐☐ ☐☐☐☐

Phone ☐☐☐   ☐☐☐   ☐☐☐☐   Fax ☐☐☐   ☐☐☐   ☐☐☐☐

Company Name ☐☐☐☐☐☐☐☐☐☐☐☐☐☐☐☐☐☐☐☐☐

E-mail address ☐☐☐☐☐☐☐☐☐☐☐☐☐☐☐☐☐☐☐☐☐☐☐☐

1. Please check at least (3) influencing factors for purchasing this book.

Front or back cover information on book .... ☐
Special approach to the content .... ☐
Completeness of content .... ☐
Author's reputation .... ☐
Publisher's reputation .... ☐
Book cover design or layout .... ☐
Index or table of contents of book .... ☐
Price of book .... ☐
Special effects, graphics, illustrations .... ☐
Other (Please specify): _____ ☐

2. How did you first learn about this book?

Internet Site .... ☐
Saw in Macmillan Computer
　Publishing catalog .... ☐
Recommended by store personnel ...... ☐
Saw the book on bookshelf at store ..... ☐
Recommended by a friend .... ☐
Received advertisement in the mail .... ☐
Saw an advertisement in: _____ ☐
Read book review in: _____ ☐
Other (Please specify): _____ ☐

3. How many computer books have you purchased in the last six months?

This book only .... ☐   3 to 5 books .... ☐
2 books .... ☐   More than 5 .... ☐

4. Where did you purchase this book?

Bookstore .... ☐
Computer Store .... ☐
Consumer Electronics Store .... ☐
Department Store .... ☐
Office Club .... ☐
Warehouse Club .... ☐
Mail Order .... ☐
Direct from Publisher .... ☐
Internet site .... ☐
Other (Please specify): .... ☐

5. How long have you been using a computer?

Less than 6 months .. ☐   6 months to a year ..... ☐
1 to 3 years .... ☐   More than 3 years ...... ☐

6. What is your level of experience with personal computers and with the subject of this book?

	With PC's	With subject of book
New	☐	☐
Casual	☐	☐
Accomplished	☐	☐
Expert	☐	☐

Source Code — ISBN: 0-7897-1491-4

7. Which of the following best describes your job title?

Administrative Assistant .... ☐
Coordinator .... ☐
Manager/Supervisor .... ☐
Director .... ☐
Vice President .... ☐
President/CEO/COO .... ☐
Lawyer/Doctor/Medical Professional ..... ☐
Teacher/Educator/Trainer .... ☐
Engineer/Technician .... ☐
Consultant .... ☐
Not employed/Student/Retired .... ☐
Other (Please specify): .... ☐

8. Which of the following best describes the area of the company your job title falls under?

Accounting .... ☐
Engineering .... ☐
Manufacturing .... ☐
Marketing .... ☐
Operations .... ☐
Sales .... ☐
Other (Please specify): .... ☐

9. What is your age?

Under 20 .... ☐
21-29 .... ☐
30-39 .... ☐
40-49 .... ☐
50-59 .... ☐
60-over .... ☐

10. Are you:

Male .... ☐
Female .... ☐

11. Which computer publications do you read regularly? (Please list)

_____
_____
_____
_____
_____
_____
_____
_____
_____

Comments: _____
_____
_____

Fold here and scotch-tape to ma